Prisons of Our mind and the Road to Freedom

Dr. John Mathai MBBS, FRANZCP, FRCPSYCH

PSYCHOLOGICAL AND SPIRITUAL INSIGHTS, OF A PERSONAL JOURNEY IN UNDERSTANDING THE WORKINGS OF THE MIND.

Foreword by Selwyn Hughes
An internationally acclaimed speaker and widely published author

Prisons of Our Mind and the Road to Freedom

ALL RIGHTS RESERVED. NO PART OF THIS PUBLICATION MAY BE REPRODUCED, STORED IN A RETRIEVAL SYSTEM OR TRANSMITTED IN ANY FORM OR BY ANY MEANS, WITHOUT THE PRIOR WRITTEN PERMISSION OF THE COPYRIGHT HOLDER, DR. JOHN MATHAI.

ISBN 1-4116-0859-3

First published in 2004

TO DAWN, JARED AND SEAN
my champions in the faith of our Lord Jesus Christ

Contents

FOREWORD	11
PREFACE	13
PSYCHOLOGICAL INSIGHTS	14
♦ Mental phenomena	14
♦ Defence mechanisms	15
♦ Communication	16
♦ Feelings and communication	18
♦ Regression and feelings	19
♦ Children and parents	20
♦ The Child and Family	21
♦ Deprived children	22
♦ Emotional pain	22
♦ Issues and feelings	23
♦ Punitive superego	24
♦ Roles	25
♦ Groups	25
♦ Splits and togetherness	25
♦ Projections	26
♦ Projective identification	27
♦ Anger	27
♦ Anxiety - Man's Worst Enemy	28
♦ Reactions	30
♦ Masks	30
♦ Relationships	31
♦ Perceptions	32
♦ Victims	32
♦ Adolescence	33
♦ Adolescent rebellion	34
♦ The Anorexic Stance	34

- ♦ Change — 36
- ♦ Systems change — 37
- ♦ Knowledge and change — 37
- ♦ Organisations and change — 37
- ♦ Family therapy — 38
- ♦ Systems theory — 38
- ♦ The larger picture — 38
- ♦ Solutions — 39
- ♦ Creating difference — 39
- ♦ Celebrate difference — 40
- ♦ Problem solving — 41
- ♦ Asking questions — 41

Psychological and Spiritual insights — 43

- ♦ Anger and anxiety/depression — 43
- ♦ Change — 44
- ♦ Wisdom — 45
- ♦ The Lord is in control — 46
- ♦ Voices of the past — 48
- ♦ Imprisoned by our past — 49
- ♦ Deprive old patterns of attention — 49
- ♦ Changing old patterns — 50
- ♦ Issues — 51
- ♦ Whole body filling — 52
- ♦ Secrets — 52
- ♦ Independence and serving one another — 53
- ♦ Feelings — 54
- ♦ Coming in touch with ones feelings — 54
- ♦ Knowledge of man is limited — 56
- ♦ Belief systems — 56
- ♦ Unity in ones belief system — 59
- ♦ Emptiness — 60
- ♦ Being one — 60
- ♦ Introspection — 61
- ♦ Roles — 62

- ♦ Thoughts — 63
- ♦ Dealing with negative thoughts — 63
- ♦ Theories and theories — 63
- ♦ Faith in Jesus Christ — 64
- ♦ Defences — 65
- ♦ Children and defences — 65
- ♦ Defensiveness — 65
- ♦ Freedom in Christ — 66
- ♦ Relationships — 67
- ♦ Self centred life style — 67
- ♦ Religions of the world — 68
- ♦ Sanctification — 69
- ♦ Old self and self — 70
- ♦ Interdependency — 71
- ♦ Coping — 71
- ♦ Experience — 73
- ♦ False guilt — 74
- ♦ Facing your fears — 75
- ♦ Superficial need vs. deeper needs — 76
- ♦ Emotionally free — 78
- ♦ Becoming what you imagine — 79
- ♦ Head and heart unity — 80
- ♦ True integration — 81
- ♦ Expectations — 81
- ♦ Fantasy and idealised relationships — 82
- ♦ Character building — 83
- ♦ Motivation — 84
- ♦ Acceptance — 85
- ♦ Acceptance of self and others — 85
- ♦ Labelling — 86
- ♦ Sin — 87
- ♦ Opening up to Gods resources — 87
- ♦ Self esteem — 88
- ♦ The neurotics prison — 89
- ♦ Addictions — 90
- ♦ Friendship — 90
- ♦ Influences — 91

- Security — 91
- Attitudes — 92
- Positive attitude — 92
- Change of attitude — 93
- Mind sets — 94
- Think — 95
- Positive thinking — 95
- Perceptions — 96
- Paradigms shifts — 97
- Confidence in self — 98
- Believe in yourself — 99
- Leaders — 99
- Resistance to change — 100
- Conflict — 100
- Strategy — 101
- Frames of reference — 102
- Problem solving — 103
- Faith overcomes fear — 103
- Conformity — 104
- Prosperity — 105
- Love key to release — 105
- Programming for success — 106
- Stop judging others — 107
- Opinions — 107
- Fixed in purpose — 107
- Pressing on — 108
- Integrate your values with your goals — 109
- Unblocking the flow — 110
- God is in control — 111
- Success in God — 111
- Preparing for success — 112
- Emotional Problems — 113
- Integrity — 113
- Don't despair — 114
- Loving self, loving others — 115
- Friendship — 116
- Persistence — 117

- Helping others to help themselves — 117
- Problems as opportunities — 118
- Laughter — 119
- Reactions — 120
- The system binds — 120
- Goal setting — 121
- Investing in others — 122
- Change — 122
- Family first — 123
- Focusing on solutions — 123
- Operating in faith — 124
- Habits — 124
- Going beyond the problems — 125
- Loving others-judging their thoughts — 125
- Love, faith and sex — 126
- Powerful change induction — 127
- Love gives and gives — 128
- Giving as sowing — 129
- Childhood experiences — 130
- Significance and love — 130
- Difference and beauty — 131
- Prayer and imagination — 132
- Self centered to other centered — 133
- Praying in tongues — 134
- The Lord is my Shepherd — 134
- Empowered from within — 135
- Faith in action — 136
- Depending on God for all things — 136
- Hitting rock bottom — 136
- Two competing forces — 137
- Total dependence on God — 137
- Maturity — 138
- Connecting behaviours and emotions — 139
- Emotional independence — 140

SPIRITUAL INSIGHTS — **141**

- Gods love — 141
- Live in the now — 147
- In Christ — 147
- Rest in Christ — 149
- Nuggets of Truth — 150
- Christ our reference point — 152
- Jesus - our standard — 154
- On being — 155
- Seeing with the eyes of Jesus — 155
- Identifications — 156
- New life in Jesus — 156
- Repentance key to forgiveness — 156
- Gods salvation — 157
- Seeking Gods way — 158
- Affirmation — 158
- False self and feelings — 158
- Sin and repentance — 159
- Sin of introspection — 159
- Sin and salvation — 160
- Saintliness and sinfulness — 160
- Sinful flesh — 161
- Sin controls you — 161
- Crucify the flesh — 162
- Keep to the right — 163
- Voices of the past — 163
- Liberty in Jesus — 164
- Suffering — 164
- Contentment — 165
- Jesus is Lord — 167
- Truth is in a person — 167
- Forces of good and evil — 168
- Selfishness — 170
- Personal relationship with God — 172
- His life – not beliefs — 173
- Cross and salvation — 173
- Principles of the Kingdom — 174
- Word of God — 176

- Adam's sin - Jesus death — 176
- Man is a spirit being — 177
- Taking up ones cross — 178
- Power of the tongue — 179
- The power of the Cross — 179
- Trinity working together — 180
- Faith in the glorified life of Christ — 180
- Remedy — 181
- Faith in God — 182
- Heavenly wisdom — 183
- Attachment to God — 183
- Hearing Gods now voice — 184
- Battles — 184
- Destiny — 184
- Jesus Christ and Him crucified — 185
- Satanic arrows — 185
- Humility — 186
- Love and humility — 187
- Holy Spirit — 188
- Prayer power — 189
- Prayer — 190
- Visualisation — 190
- Faith — 191
- Holy Spirit the conductor — 191
- Imagination — 192
- Faith imagination — 193
- Love — 193
- Love is above difference — 195
- Investing in others — 195
- Victorious living — 195
- Bondage — 196
- God is in control — 196
- Creator God — 197
- Prayer of renunciation — 198
- Gratefulness — 198
- Self sacrifice — 199
- Yoked to Christ — 200

- Abundant living — 201
- Trust in God — 202
- Moving in faith — 203
- Walking in the spirit — 205
- Faith walk — 205
- Walking with Jesus — 206
- Giving till it hurts — 207
- Breaking through — 207
- Speaking Gods truth in love — 208
- Faith in self in God — 208
- Vision — 209
- Sanctifying our bodies daily for the Holy Spirit — 210
- Overcoming faith — 210
- Discerning the spirit — 211
- Values — 212
- Choices — 213
- Christ in me — 213
- Prophetic word — 214
- Changed into His image — 214
- Death brings life into focus — 215
- Synchronise the inner and outer life — 215
- Balance in all areas — 216
- Worship — 217
- Defensiveness cripples — 217
- Heavenly manna — 218
- Reach out for more — 219
- Open to the Spirit — 220
- Total abandonment to the Lord — 221
- Transparency — 222
- Surrender to Jesus-key to exorcise demon of control — 223
- Purity — 224
- Converting you negatives into positives — 226
- **Index** — **228**

FOREWORD

How I wish I had access to this book when I first began my ministry in counselling. It is a veritable mine of psychological and spiritual information that will reward any reader, whether he or she is a professional counsellor or just someone who wants to know more about the workings of the human mind.

The genius of the book is the way it integrates the best of psychological insights with a Christian perspective. In my experience psychologists who are Christians often view Biblical truths through the lens of psychology rather than viewing psychology through the lens of Scripture. Dr Mathai clearly brings all his thinking to the judgment bar of Scripture and ensures that all he says is in harmony with the truths that lie within the Word of God. It is refreshing to find a psychiatrist who speaks so freely and openly about his faith and how it has helped him in his own quest for maturity.

I have been fascinated and intrigued when reading through the manuscript at how brief statements leap out and hit home with powerful and memorable accuracy. Startling sentences pop up on almost every page that will inscribe themselves in the memory and continuously call forth the reader into a new understanding of oneself, others and of course, God.

Here are just a few `tasters' that will help you prepare for the banquet that lies ahead:

> Having a good self esteem ...does not mean a rejection of dependence on God. Self esteem is to live comfortably with one self... to accept myself as I am.

> The secret of friendship is the ability to think and feel for others.

> The greatest discovery of this century is that change of attitude leads to change of behaviour
>
> If I love myself then I will want the best for myself...I will want to bless others. My responses to others are just a reflection of how I feel about myself.
>
> The tough times will not last. God's power is released when tough times turn people into tough people.
>
> Love, faith and sex are all linked together. Therefore don't be surprised that each is stimulated in your relationships.

Believe me there are many, many more.

Dr John's writing is powerful not only because of his training but also a lifetime of experience in people helping. I am so glad that he has made accessible to us the wisdom he has gained over the years.

I hope to spend many hours dipping into this book and expect to profit from it every time I open its pages. I think that you will experience this also.

Selwyn Hughes
Waverley Abbey House,
Farnham, Surrey, England,
U.K

Preface

I have attempted in this book to record the collection of thoughts, ideas, revelations and insights I have received over 30 years of my professional life. I have been fascinated by the stories I have heard from my patients over the years. I have felt the pain and anguish of souls struggling with the confusion of feelings and thoughts as they attempt to understand and free themselves from their inner pain. I too have struggled in my personal life with this pain. I am grateful to my patients who have trusted me over the years in revealing the dark side of their self so that I could understand their pain. This is not an easy thing to do. They made themselves vulnerable hoping that in this process they could be delivered or freed from their inner pain and suffering. I have come to realise that this kind of pain is the worse form of pain any human being could suffer. I have tried to be of help to them through the knowledge and experience I have gained over the years. Yet knowledge alone did not seem to be enough most of the time to answer all the questions and solve all the problems. The treatment was able to bring some relief from suffering. This I believe was in the form of empathy and understanding of the pain of the other. I don't make any claim that I have all the answers. I only want to share my insights hoping that this will be a source of strength and encouragement to others that are also on the same journey of discovery and adventure.

I have over the years been exposed to many theories and approaches all of which I have found had something to say. I am grateful to my teachers through these many works of literature. Most of all I have, I believe, received these revelations and insights through a personal and daily walk with my Lord and Saviour Jesus Christ. To Him I give all glory and praise for the gift of understanding and the wisdom to know what to do, to help others help themselves. I trust the reader will be blessed as I have been over the years in reading and absorbing these revelations.

Dr. John Mathai MBBS, FRANZCP, FRCPsych
Consultant Psychiatrist, Melbourne, Australia

PSYCHOLOGICAL INSIGHTS

These insights are examples of how we deal with our feelings at a psychological level. They are an attempt to try and understand how our mind tends to respond to psychological threat.

MENTAL PHENOMENA

Mental phenomena are illusory and are related to internal states. The mind begins to fantasise and work through the feelings generated through threat, fear and anxiety. The mind can cope only by projecting those fears to particular persons in the present as this allows for problem solving. It is your mind that is doing it, but in the game, there are accusers or blamers, and victims or placaters. You can either identify with the victim or blamer.

This kind of game playing is usually in preparation for what you have to deal with before you. Most of the time these feelings are generated in you through your own fears and anxieties, and have nothing to do with the real persons outside. However, this process highlights your own mental state and equilibrium. It only distorts the reality of the situation, and causes you to come to wrong conclusions, which lead to wrong decisions because of tackling it to appease yourself, that is your inner child that is threatened. This leads to rigidity and control.

On the other hand living in the now enables you to live in the present now and not in the future past. That is, if you are always living in what is to be, you fail to live in the present now and the future is usually different from what you conceived it would be. This is living by vain imagination's, or illusions.

Living in the now is to feel and experience the now and ever present and the past and future are irrelevant. Living in your dreams is unreal and illusory- it serves to keep you static and bound. No growth occurs, as this is defensive living and not productive.

The power you have is wasted in illusory phenomena and not

directed to the now. Most people live this way and waste their lives and energy in goalless pursuits that end in getting nowhere. Living in the now is to feel in the present and be active in doing and thinking and feeling now. This is to be known and to know. This will give you a strong sense of identity and purpose.

DEFENCE MECHANISMS

Defence means withdrawal. One can never advance in defence. Either one stays fixed in one place or moves backwards. Defences keep one safe from hurt but it does not enable one to feel. The defence is a protection against hurtful emotions. The emotions are generated within a person - mainly negative in times of crisis. One then goes into defence to protect oneself from those hurtful feelings. It's usually loved ones that are able to stir up these feelings for our defences are most vulnerable in the midst of those we know. Outsiders can hurt but because they are unknowns they do not have a big capacity to hurt as much as the ones we know. Especially the ones we love and depend on have the maximum capacity to bring out hurtful feelings. It's our reactions that hurt. It's not so much what others say or do that matter but our own responses. These responses can come from any position. In families they are mainly childhood responses. Emotions that have become stuck at that level are aroused in certain circumstances. A mature person is able to identify them as such and not to react to them. A person unaware of these states quickly gets overwhelmed and blames the person who was the instigator or provoker of these feelings. So a dependant person becomes overwhelmed with anger when the person they look up to opposes them or corrects them. Fear takes over and the dependent person is caught in the midst of contradictory emotions of fear and hatred. Fear of loosing the object of their love and hatred for making them feel that way. Maturity is to take responsibility for these feelings and to label them as such, as feelings are aroused. When labelled, they lose the power to overwhelm and defence becomes less necessary. One can learn from these feelings. To feel is to live.

When one is cut off at the heart level, life becomes boring, rigid and monotonous - like a robot. Life is to be lived and this means operating from the heart - the head providing the limits. Children out of control are living on their feelings of fear, hurt, rejection, loss and their head has lost control. Inhibited children have suppressed their feelings by over control and so appear like adults. Their feelings overwhelm them but they have converted their negative feelings into worry and anxiety/depression - they have internalised them. They suffer a great toll because of this and this affects their relationships. The way out is for them to relax and let go. This means to become as a child and to let go of the need to control. To be able to feel again and not feel bad or fearful and then to be able to obtain control. To feel secure within and not be moved by circumstances but to rule from within.

COMMUNICATION

There are two types of communication - one is logical, rational and problem solving and the other is emotional or affective. If two people are communicating and are doing so at different levels, then there will be a lack of communication, or mis-communication occurs. When people switch from one level to the other, then there is scope for misunderstanding to occur.
Friendships, relationships are built on the second kind of communication, which is more to do with sharing one's thoughts and feelings, which may then aid problem-solving.
Clarification of these two kinds of communication will free up communication. Usually if there is a problem in the first then there is a problem in the second. In most relationships there is either a confusion of the two, or a lack in the second. Conflicts occur when one partner switches from one level to another. This is a kind of defence or block. So if there is a defensive block on the emotional side, then this will give rise to difficulties in problem solving, or a problem solving issue turns into an emotional conflict.
In families too this kind of mis-communication occurs and this gives rise to conflicts and indecision and the family or system gets stuck.

In work situations the first kind of communication occurs. In social and family relationships it is the second kind that occurs. However, if there is a lack of it in experience then there needs to be practice. Lack of it leads usually to poverty in relationships. Those who are poor attract others who are poor. Like attracts like. A man is known by his friends.

A scientific, materialistic age usually looks down on emotional communication, but ignoring it is to one's detriment. A man who is able to distinguish the two and not be threatened by either is mature. It is when the two are allowed to influence each other that a true sense of being occurs; otherwise a person feels split off, one minute operating rationally and the next irrationally. It is when the head does not check emotions that they go wild.

A person who is not experienced in handling feelings will find it threatening. He therefore exercises excessive control over them. In this way he appears to be rather cold and calculating. A person who is free is able to feel and move freely with others and make contact at a feeling level with others. The spiritual realm is one further step where one is able to communicate with God, spirit to spirit. All three levels of communication are important. Too much emphasis on one level leads to imbalance. All three should be able to inform each other and thus lead to balance. The ability to function on all three levels leads to wholeness.

Being proactive means that one is on top. So I need to be there doing the stuff. One must be able to put oneself in the shoes of the other to be able to know how the other thinks so that whatever strategy is used are cognisant of the others' mode of thinking. Then operating in the other's mode enables communication to take place. The ability to shift from one mode to another is the key to successful communication. If one is stuck in one mode of communication then not only is one deprived but also communication is blocked. This kind of rigidity in thinking is what leads to a constricted personality. So the key to freeing oneself is to experiment in different ways of thinking, feeling and action. Using the different senses - visual, hearing, touch, also aids in communication. The aim is to free people up to think and operate in different modes so that the world is perceived through different ways. This will enable the brain to use different modes to solve problems. If one is stuck in one way or limited number of ways then creativity is reduced and so the ability to have access to solutions is also reduced. So respecting, listening, using other's perceptions enables one to experiment in different ways of seeing and doing leading to an ability to be malleable, adaptable and to see the situation from a parent's point of view, child's point of view and outsider's point of view and come to a new level of understanding and problem solving. Conflict arises when the paradigms are in conflict. The shift occurs when paradigms shift or understanding of the other's paradigm leads to empathy, leading to solutions.

FEELINGS AND COMMUNICATION

Feelings if not acknowledged and confessed have a sneaky way of controlling one's behaviour. It is not others who determine your behaviour but your response to the words and actions of others. If you fail to acknowledge your feelings, your feelings will then distort the reality, and put the blame on others. Maturity is to be able to accept yourself, feelings, weaknesses and strengths. Feelings are not good or bad. They make you the person you are, that is able to feel pain and joy. Feelings are not facts. They come and go and therefore decisions cannot be based on them. However, they are able to confirm or aid in decision-making. If feelings are not acknowledged, then you are denying or rejecting a part of you. If you do this, then you give control to that feeling, or feel uncomfortable with that feeling generated in you. One way to deal with feelings is to address them, and to hear what they are saying to you, to aid you in your communications. If you ignore them, then you are depriving yourself of valuable information that would diminish or deprive you of good judgment. A person who is able to accept his feelings and address them is also a person who is in charge of himself. When one does this, there is less likelihood for those feelings to dictate your behaviour. Once acknowledged, your feelings will be under your conscious control.

REGRESSIONS AND FEELINGS

Regressions lead to childhood feelings being experienced in the present. This can be threatening but also an opportunity to be able to heal yourself. If those feelings were denied or handled by other ways than by acceptance, then you will be plagued by those feelings until your dying day, that is feelings are tied to memories. Feelings keep those memories alive. Negative feelings related to or connected to negative memories will continue to influence your life and self-esteem. Unless those feelings are addressed they are like a threat within you. Confessing them is like dealing with those feelings so that they are no more a threat to you. To be free emotionally is to be free from the threat of those feelings that bind you to a way of living and coping that keep you constricted as an individual. So do not allow your feelings to dictate your behaviour responses, but acknowledge your feelings, that is, confess them so that you can be set free from their tyrannical rule over your life.

It is easier to label people rather than look at the relationship. Labelling is a regressive phenomenon, a form of scapegoating. Always look at the relationship and this will lead to better problem solving and relationships.

Whenever conflict arises, it is easier to label than look at what is happening in the relationship and how anxiety levels lead to regressions and defensive behaviour that lead to fight or flight responses.

People are trapped by their feelings. Listen and identify those feelings and then help them to release themselves from their power. Name them first and then help them to voice them. As they voice them they are spitting it out of their mouths. By naming them one is released from their power. Denying them causes them to control one's life. They then play games. Identify the emotion that controls a group and then address them. It is as the group addresses these feelings, that they are released to function. This is part of therapy, which leads to growth. It is not personalities but issues that need to be addressed.

CHILDREN AND PARENTS

Children can be used as punching bags for one's own negative emotions. The best way to deal with one's negativity is to confess it and own it. In a therapy situation, individuals must be enabled to express their emotions and their thoughts together. The patient may put the therapist in a parent, adult or child role. The feelings will also be according to the role one is in. Such transferences are linked to early relationships towards authority figures, for example, parent, siblings, others. It is easy to label such people, but labelling those transferences allows the individual to deal with them more appropriately, otherwise it will just repeat itself in other relationships. The key is to look for positives in others, for in this way they are made less defensive, and therefore encourage the revelation of their negative selves that have crippled them from leading a full life.

Children react to the atmosphere they are in. A loving, understanding and helpful environment will enable them to grow. A critical, uncertain and selfish environment will stunt them, and make them defensive. Where the adults are taken up with their own careers or ambitions, there is no time to create an environment for the child. The child has to relate to whoever is available. The child learns to cope on his own resources from an early age. The adults try to make up for this deprivation through gifts. What a child needs is not things but love and understanding. As the child grows and comes to terms with the environment, she needs a secure base to explore her world. It is the parents that provide the base. It is the relationship with the parents that the child's relationships in the future are built on. A poor marital relationship will give rise to children having difficulty trusting relationships, or produce guilt-ridden relationships. A secure child is not caught up with these feelings of guilt and suspicion.

When people have their ups and downs, to be able to hold them is essential for their security. Parents who react or feel rejected are unable to provide those limits. Child and parents who are similar in characteristics will read into each other, and will find distancing or separation difficult because they are bound to each other by their mutual projections. Maturity is to know one's boundaries, and be able to maintain those boundaries in a relationship.

THE CHILD AND FAMILY

The child in the womb experiences the feelings of his mother. That is why the mental health of the mother is so important to the health of the child.

The child needs love if it is to survive. Feelings are real. They cannot be ignored. One's feelings are contained in a secure and predictable environment. The environment of a child is its family. Initially it is his mother that is the child's environment. This is why attachment to the mother is so important. If a mother is unable to care, then any person who is able to provide care for the child is good enough. The important and vital ingredient is love that enables the child to be attached emotionally; to receive the nourishment that only a human being can give. Each child is an individual, and his needs have to be catered for until he is able to fend for himself. When his needs are not met, then he will continue to see his fulfilment through others.

Our fear of authority figures is very much related to our relationship to our parents. If they were punitive, undermining and paralysing, then we will project these images on to others in authority positions. This is also reflected in our image of God our Father. Adolescence is especially a period of finding one's own identity. This process is in coming to terms with one's own ability to decide to function as an individual without the fear of being told off. If there is an incomplete resolution of this, then there will continue to be difficulties with authority figures. Authority is seen as the superego. If one subjects oneself to an authority figure, then one feels dependent on that person, which arouses feelings of ambivalence, that is, hate and love. Hate leads to guilt, which is then responded to by being over-solicitous, or passively aggressive, that is, indirectly being undermining. An unhealthy respect of authority figures leads to an overt rebellion towards them that prevents healthy working through i.e., always looking for weaknesses rather than respecting authority figures for who they are and the roles they are in. Both reactions are unhealthy and are a reaction of one's own hang-ups towards authority figures. These projections need to be handled in such a way that it does not undermine and lead to chaos and confusion.

Young people need authority figures. This enables them to feel safe. Their own aggressive impulses threaten to overwhelm them, and a healthy respect for authority enables them to feel safe. Care and authority need to be seen together. Limits are caring responses. However, an adult needs to exercise his/her own limits. It is in the formation of a personality that adults need to set standards so that the young person feels safe to work out his/her own quest for a sense of self and identity.

DEPRIVED CHILDREN

Children who are rejected and deprived continue to elicit rejection by their demands on their carers who they exhaust. They are unable to control their hostile feelings to the love object because of past deprivation and rejection. The rejections they elicit from their love object further reinforces
their feelings of unlove which cages them. Some children can split off this part which therefore only acts out in certain situations.

EMOTIONAL PAIN

Pain is an illusion of the real. Pain restricts one's thinking and feeling. Emotional pain is converted into physical pain. Release is through acknowledging how the pain aids one's functioning, that is, serves a purpose, to find more effective ways in coping with one's feelings, by confession, forgiveness and restitution. When you move away from the individual and concentrate on issues, then it is possible to look for solutions. Concentrating on changing the individual leads to labelling, introspection and stuckness. Looking at issues brings it out in the open and enables problem solving. This also distances the problem from the individual and there is less chance of being labelled, paralysed and constricted.

ISSUES AND FEELINGS

An issue has other sounds to it. Until the basic issue is tackled, then other issues become contentious arenas for conflict. The basic issue may be to do with perceived powerlessness and therefore an issue of confidentiality
becomes contentious. It is important to then define the issue and address the feelings. When feelings cloud the issue it becomes too difficult to resolve it. Feelings are personal and each individual brings to an issue his/her feelings, which have personal roots, embedded in past experience which colours current perception. Feelings interfere with current functioning but when addressed for what they are, just feelings, not fact, then they can be acknowledged and decisions can then be made on the facts of the situation.
It is good to address feelings because these block problem solving. Feelings of anger and jealousy are destructive. They need to be addressed; otherwise they will cloud one's thinking. Feelings make one think in very concrete terms. This is frustrating as the issue is not to do with X causing Y, but more to do with attitudes. Sometimes addressing the feelings allows the issue to be separated from the feelings and the issue ceases to be an issue.
When a subject becomes an issue about power, then the subject takes on new parameters. A simple issue of bedtime may be more to do with one's identity or survival, rather than whether it is 8pm or 9pm. Addressing feelings therefore are as important as addressing the topic. When people are acknowledged and their opinions listened to and respected, there is less chance for conflict. Self-acceptance or [lack of it] is the basis for a lot of conflicts. Scapegoating, splitting, displacement, are all defence mechanisms that are employed to distance oneself from the feelings, but they are not helpful to growth and good working relationships. Do not label others but look at helpful solutions.

PUNITIVE SUPEREGO

A punitive superego suppresses the ego, which then is anxious and fearful.
The anger, which is aroused, is then converted into anxiety, fear, confusion and depression, which further damages the ego and results in low self-esteem. A punitive superego is developed because of past experience with authority figures - severe, cold and uncaring. Rejections in the present then interfere with relationships. Feelings are aroused and it is easier to give in, but at a cost. In giving in, anger and guilt sets in which then affects self-esteem. A person who lives to pacify his superego lives by the law of words. A punitive superego cannot trust others and therefore controls them and restricts their development. A punitive superego plays subversive games and makes others angry. It is not what others think of you but what you think of yourself that matters. What others think of you is just a reflection of what you think of yourself. You project an image of yourself to others that is received or perceived by others. This may not be based on fact - and usually is not - people are deceived by the outward. People project a more positive picture than is, for everyone loves to be appreciated and liked. However, unless what is projected is synchronous with what is felt there will be a disharmony in perception and this incongruity will be the basis for confused reactions. A person who is able to accept the positive and negative aspects of himself is able to accept these in others. A person who is able to accept only the positive and reject the negative does this in others too. We do unto others what we do unto ourselves. If we can't accept our own weakness and prejudices then we will not be able to tolerate these in others. Our response to others is just a reflection of our likes and dislikes. It's the need to be liked, to appear successful that are reflections of a deprived soul. To be relaxed with one's self is to be at peace. I do not need to compare myself with others for my security and significance does not depend on others but on myself.

ROLES

The separation between roles in one's own personal life is artificial, just like the clothes one wears on oneself. Behind every role is a person. Sometimes one relates to the role and the feelings aroused are in relation to that role. Reactions are sometimes aroused in relation to that particular role and not to the person. If these are not separated the feelings towards the role become or are perceived as personal attacks, whereas in actual fact it is towards that specific role.
At home the person rather than the role is more prominent and one is not playing a role like when at a job. It is more difficult to play a role at home because the gap between the person and the role is much less. It is easy to hide behind a role. However the feelings that are aroused are related to the person behind the role. How one exercises one's role is related to the person. The role is to enable one to perform functions. However, there is a person behind the role who has feelings, and must be respected, not for the role, but for the person he or she is, a human being.
Unemployment results in a person without a work role. Because men are more attuned to work, such a role outside the home is very important to his sense of self.

GROUPS

Difficulty in groups arises because one's boundaries are threatened due to poor ego strength, or sense of self, which is threatened. When a group regresses to labelling individuals, or scapegoating, it is to distract from what is happening in the group. The more similar in nature the group is, the more inward looking and regressed it will be. Variety enables the group to adapt to change and strengthens the group.

SPLITS AND TOGETHERNESS

Splits cause one to see things in one way. Togetherness causes us to see things our way. This changes perceptions. United we look to bind and bond. Separated we seek to defend and seek our own way - to win. United we have to win together. Everything that keeps us together is what we will seek to do. Anything that separates us we will forego.

PROJECTIONS

The object to whom you direct your lusts and feelings is turned into a receptacle of your negative thoughts and feelings and becomes such. They are then diminished into a thing and no more respected as a person. Likewise a person can also be endued with a lot of positives and revered like a god invested with power above what is expected. These projections of yourself on to others then influence your perceptions, which lead to transferences - positive and negative, that elicit in the other negative or positive behaviours.

These projections are below the surface of consciousness and occur in all relationships especially the intimate ones. In these situations, projections are acted out and in the process the past is acted out linked to the person's relationships with past objects- good or bad. Transferences of a negative type are linked to past experiences with present figures that elicit responses that either confirm or disconfirm present relationships. One way to cope with this is to distance oneself but this only leads to poverty in relationships at a considerable cost. Working through these conflicts, thoughts and feelings is a more painful process but is a healing process. The first step in this process is to acknowledge one's own feelings and to be in touch with them. Not to analyse them but to be in touch with them.

Being in touch with them enables one to feel more a person and to take responsibility for them. This will then enable one to project less and frees one in relationship with another. Positive and negative transferences take place in all relationships. It's when a person is able to cope with both and keep them in balance that results in wholeness.

PROJECTIVE IDENTIFICATION

When parents project their angry and hostile feelings onto the child and the child identifies with these feelings and acts up, the parent then corrects the child and in the process calms himself and the child's guilt is relieved through punishment, but there is the state of blurring of boundaries and therefore lack of differentiation of self from the other.

ANGER

Anger is a basic emotion. The expression of it is determined by the varying degrees of repression that it is confronted with during development. The less secure the limits to contain anger, the more infantile its expression. Anger aroused is then freely expressed without any control.
Limits, which are not sufficiently applied during a child's growth, create difficulties due to disruption of family life. The child then becomes the source of a lot of attention, which distracts the family from other needs. This leads to arousal of anger in the members towards this particular child who has lack of anger control. This could lead to rejection and scapegoating of the child and ultimate expulsion. When the child is first expelled, it initially gives a sense of peace to the rest of the family but soon tensions arise again to fight for attention for each other's neglected needs, or the conflict shifts to another area, for example, the marital relationship. This may then lead to the return of the child home again, to hold the marriage together. It is easier to dump one's anger on someone else, than to own responsibility for it. A family that does not have clear boundaries promotes misunderstandings due to unclear communication.
No one listens and the most disruptive member receives the most attention at the expense of the rest. This is contained in the family till the child enters school. This may be the first crisis where the child finds that the environment rejects its behaviour. This may be the first time the child is referred for

help. The child then becomes the elected patient to obtain help for the family.

Anger that is sufficiently repressed leads to its expression through anxiety fear and depression. These are all expressions of anger, which gives rise to subjective feelings of anxiety, fear and depression with its physiological components. The mind has developed sufficient control, but then expresses itself by moderating its expression through these symptoms, which receive attention and sympathy from others. Such a child also arouses anger in others, which is also repressed, and therefore only fuels the anxiety or fear. It may also convert into physical symptoms. Physical symptoms occur through the mental mechanism of splitting, which then converts the emotion into a physical symptom. The individual concerned is oblivious of the fact of the emotions, since it is isolated into a specific symptom. All the distress is due to the physical symptoms. Individuals who operate through denial and projective mechanisms are able to split off emotions from the self, so they are not distressed by it. On the other hand they cause a lot of distress in others who care for them. Treating the symptom as something alien enables the individual to distance himself from the symptom, but does not change the basic mechanism that gave rise to it in the first place. Again integration of the personality is called for through taking personal responsibility for these emotions, the owning of them and the integration into oneself.

ANXIETY - MAN'S WORST ENEMY

Anxiety gives rise to feelings of discomfort is healthy, because it stimulates us into taking anticipatory action to deal with the anxiety-provoking situation. However, a lot of the anxiety one feels is imagined, or due to how we perceive ourselves, or how we think others see us. How we perceive ourselves is very much related to the concept of self. If we have a poor self-image, then we are mainly thinking negative self-damnatory thoughts about ourselves. These thoughts which have been around for a long time are usually much more to the fore in crisis situations. When everything is going well then these thoughts are in the background. Many of these thoughts have a familiar pattern; that is, they say the same things. Our perception of our self also reflects on how we present ourselves to others. This will lead to how others will perceive us, or have an influence on how others will perceive us. Therefore whether the source of the anxiety is from within or without, ultimately the process of assessment will lead one to consider how the information is processed by an individual which ultimately will lead to feelings of anxiety, panic or depression. These thought patterns have more or less a life of their own, because they are automatic, as if on automatic pilot. Therapy will be aimed at identifying these automatic thoughts, so that familiar thought patterns can be identified. When these thought patterns are identified, then they can be confronted for what they are in the light of cold reality, and their power over one destroyed or modified.

The process is therefore an event/thought, which leads to automatic thoughts, leading to arousal of feelings. If this is the case then it is important to try and elicit from the child or the adult how they perceive situations. Usually an individual develops a repertoire of defences to cope with these thoughts.

Therefore there will be a distortion of reality because of the defences used to cope with the anxiety. The type of defences used will be very much related to one's developmental level, as well as the defences that are most effective in containing anxiety. Denial and projections is the most primitive of the defences, but also handicaps an individual to a level of coping, which is immature and leads to a lot of stress in the environment he lives in. Such an individual is unaware of the extent of stress he or she is causing to others he/she lives with.

Other more mature defences allow a person to be more aware of others, and therefore are more amenable to accept correction, and therefore change.

One of the ways to bring about change could be to educate people in more mature ways of managing anxiety. Anxiety always implies threat of some kind. Whether it is from the boss or from colleagues or from within. Ultimately it is seen or perceived as a threatening situation.

Communication is a very important channel for anxiety management. It helps to manage and to come to terms with a situation and one's thoughts in a constructive manner. However, it is important to be able to be honest and direct to benefit from communication. Most communication is indirect and vague, and therefore only induces more anxiety. This is why it is useful to talk to someone who is distant from the problem, which will allow for more direct and open communication. It is very difficult to communicate with someone who is perceived as a threat. Defences are up and distort the situation and therefore one is not able to confront one's thoughts more directly.

REACTIONS

It is in one's reactions that one becomes aware of one's vulnerability.
Reactions are defences against threat. This is pain. When people react they are revealing vulnerable aspects about themselves. They may appear to be taking it out on others, but it is the hurt child in them that is reacting. What they need is support and not condemnation. Once they can release themselves, then hopefully they will be able to get themselves together again.
Therapy is allowing people to come to terms with their negative selves. Unless they are given the opportunity to heal themselves, they are going to continue to project their negative parts onto others. Majoring on the positives of another allows them to confess their negatives. Even children need acknowledgment of their positives. They become difficult because too much emphasis is put on their negative behaviour, which may be a reaction to the reactions of the parent's feelings. It is important that the parents own up to their own feelings and not blame the child's behaviour for their negative feelings, for this is a form of scapegoating.

MASKS

A lot of what is seen is just a mask. The real feelings are only allowed to arise in close, confiding relationships. A lot of close relationships are held on through guilt feelings. These are bondages and produce only fear. A trusting relationship allows others to be real and accepts the other for who they are. A person who blames others has not accepted himself or herself. The only way they can accept themselves is by putting others down. The areas they put others down, are the areas they are blind to themselves. Healing comes as individuals address their own feelings. These feelings link back to childhood relationships. Those unhealed areas are acted out in present relationships. These areas are evidenced mainly in conflict. Conflict is an opportunity for healing or hurt. Conflict is an indication of pain. A person is selfish because his needs have not been met, or have been indulged in. An indulged child does not know how to give, because all he knew was how to take. A child whose needs were not met is in poverty and needs love not condemnation. True knowledge is gained through process and working through relationships.

RELATIONSHIPS

In all relationships this process occurs as people go through the process of trusting each other. Until we get to that phase it is going to involve a lot of pain, challenges and upsets. The more mature parts of us must hold on until we work through these phases and come out more whole. What is being worked through is an open and flexible system that will be able to contain all the anxieties that are generated from within and without. One cannot do this in isolation.

When I am more able to face up to my own feelings, the less uncomfortable I am with others. Because I will project fewer of my feelings onto others and therefore perceive others in a better light. This is the key to self-acceptance. The less I accept myself, the more I will blame others and the more I will feel isolated and rejected. In stressful situations there will be a tendency to blame others, as a way of coping. The need to acknowledge one's own feelings, but at the same time recognise the possibility of projected feelings allows one to move forward. If I identify with projected feelings, then it is a reaction to those feelings that confuses the victim. The reaction maybe from the other who sees his rejected feelings in me, or it can be my own reaction to the projected feeling, which if not acknowledged, will be covered up.

In over-involved families someone feels blamed and this maybe the projected feelings of others on to one individual who then is the receptacle for all the bad feelings in the family. There is therefore an atmosphere. The victim identifies with those feelings and acts them out which reinforces the belief in others that she is bad.

This is what happens when individuals do not take responsibility for their own behaviour and therefore unloads onto others. A lot of the time people cannot do much because they are reacting to perceived threats. Once someone who is moody is labelled then he/she becomes the victim, but the victim can also be the aggressor, when he/she reacts to the projections and paralyses the group, or controls the group. When one stops labelling then there is a chance of addressing the issue, or underlying feelings that could bring about movement.

PERCEPTIONS

It is one's perception that leads to conflict. It is not the person, but how we perceive the person. We make judgments on partial information. If we had more information then our perceptions would change. It is important therefore to separate the person from one's perception. Negative perceptions interfere with relationships and problem solving. Therapy aims to change our perceptions and therefore free us from the power of these negative perceptions.

VICTIMS

A victim's perceptions are negative which leads to difficult relationships of abusers and victims. Who are the victims? Change through reconciliation brings abusers and victims together to work through issues. Legal process will only increase the division and increase the likelihood of victimisation.

In a hierarchical system there is always the possibility of abuse of power, but the group should stabilise matters by ensuring the forum for the expression of feelings. The group should be aware of any such polarisation of positions and attempt to see one another's position honestly.

The group should facilitate the expression of feelings and deal with the phenomenon like splitting, displacements, projections, etc, so that the system does not get stuck but grows.

ADOLESCENCE

Adolescence is about independence, breaking free and being self-sufficient. In the process there is a part that wants to be protected and another part that wants to be free. The need to be protected from others and the pain of having to stand up and be accounted, to survive on one's own financially and emotionally. The other part does not want to be free so that they can blame parents for inefficiency and lack of protection. Responsibility goes with freedom, or independence. Neurotics tend to displace and avoid conflicts mainly through projection. Confronting them with their projections leads to change, that is, taking responsibility for their behaviour [thoughts and feelings]. This leads to growth. In groups the adolescent will use the group for protection. Staff too capitalise and use the group to confront and bring about change. Adolescents confront authority because authority stands for their superego. This struggle for freedom from their superego, which could be over punitive or too lax, or confused, leads to confrontation with authority figures. The ego is trapped. Parents are the adolescent's authority figures. If parents have not been united, then the kids would have developed either a warring set of values, limits, or set up their own which is not relevant. The adolescent carries his parents wherever he goes. A good parent has a calming effect and negative parent a threatening effect. Much of the work is to engage the adolescent to change his perceptions of himself and others through the process of therapy.

ADOLESCENT REBELLION

Many influences distract young people and prey on their emotions and need for purpose and meaning. This search for something different is a way of breaking from the disillusionment with life to find something meaningful.
The resulting conflict enables the youngster to have a purpose, for it makes him feel there is something happening, as his feelings for autonomy and independence emerge and enable him to separate from what is common and known. This conflict enables the young person to make sense of himself and his world. It enables him to get in touch with his true feelings. Without this conflict he will never know himself but will live up to what others think he should do. Conflict avoidance prevents this process occurring. The conflict therefore becomes underhand and subversive and leads to physical symptoms or prolonged irritation and anxiety/depression symptoms. Conflict is part of the process of growing up and needs to be seen as such. It will be welcomed as long as it is not seen as a win/loose situation but as part of the process of growth. Too much suppression of individuality leads to rigidity and black and white thinking. To be secure in oneself means to accept all aspects of oneself and to be true to one's feelings and not reject some and accept only the positives. Rejecting the negative in oneself leads to projection and distortions that interfere with communications. Confronting those feelings in oneself and in others in a supportive/loving way leads to release and freeing of communication.

The Anorexic Stance

In anorexia the weight becomes the central issue and takes over control of the individual. Everything is centred on food, as food is what controls the weight. So fighting over food only gives more power to the weight.
Refusing to talk about food allows the individual who is controlled by weight to concentrate on other issues. The family

is also caught up in this, for they too feel that if the weight is normal, then everything else will be okay. The weight is therefore a distracter from the real issue. Weight and food are metaphors for deeper underlying feelings, to do with fear of loss of identity and angry and hostile feelings to parental figures. Mother figures as a central figure, because food is associated with nurturing and nurturing with mothers.

Central to the anorexic problem is a hatred of self and a need to punish self, and probably kill it. This then is taken out on others, who have failed to meet the needs [perceived or real] of the individual. The central core of the individual is starved of affection. She has built up her world around achievement and success is associated with receiving love and attention.

However, this does not meet her deep need to be loved. The driving force makes her into a compulsive addict to even better her performance, but in the process she blocks off everything else and concentrates her energies in work, activity and food, or the lack of it. In this state all her emotions not only drive her but also others and play havoc on relationships. All kinds of crafty devices are employed to hoodwink the other. This is to keep the outsider away and any intrusion is seen as attack. Control becomes a major issue. It is an issue of survival.

Parents need to be firm but caring. They should not give in to the constant barrage of projective feelings but stand firm in their love and care for their child who is in a struggle within herself to survive- a life and death struggle. On one hand she is controlled by weight and on the other the desire to please others. In the process she does not know who she is.

Patient and consistent management over a period of time will bring the person into themselves. Rather than being controlled by these feelings that have been suppressed for such a long time, they are freed from their power over that life. Feelings are expressed appropriately and instead of projecting is accepted as one's own and slowly the individual is freed from its power to grow in strength in body, mind and spirit. Feelings are allowed to be expressed rather than suppressed. As the individual comes into her own, then others are defined as separate from her.

Parents need support during this time, as their own sense of self is also threatened with the barrage of emotions.

Change

Change is anything that is done differently. The ability to understand the content of the problem and make a change to the content and the problem disappears. So if the problem is sustained by my perception - then a change in the way I perceive will happen as I change my action. If I am reacting to a situation then my reaction keeps me hooked to the relationship or behaviour or symptom. It is the feeling that needs to change. This feeling will change when I change my habitual responses. If I suppress my true feelings then I lie to others and myself. It is better to release myself either by being real or to change my state by taking action to change my habitual responses. One way is to entertain other possibilities. Change comes when these possibilities become avenues for new shifts in the way I perceive a person or problem. Positive impressions lead to shifts - enormous shifts. Negativity is regressive - it does not entertain creative possibilities. Therefore it keeps me stuck to a situation or problem.

One needs to have a positive mindset to be able to look at problems as opportunities. This is a shift in mental attitude.

Giving is such a blessing but it is love more than money that people need. A loving response can reap an abundance of joy.

It's not what I have but who I am that makes the difference - what I have within me.

I get blessed when I give as I can't but give.

There never will be a better time than now. The issues, problems, predicaments of today will challenge me to improve myself for tomorrow. So don't wait to be better, now is the time to be the best. Don't postpone - if you can't do it now you may never be able to do it. So give of your best. Maintain a high state of productivity by focusing on the task at hand. Cancel all other distractions and keep to the task.

Systems change

People bring their own pathology and then blame it on the system. We generate our own stress. When individual responsibility is not taken then people degenerate into a mass without individual identities. The mass is powerful but at the expense of the individual. A mature individual will have a healthy impact on the group. An immature one will just hinder the group. Should one focus on the traffic system or the mechanics or both? If the mechanics is faulty, the traffic system is no use. It is like having a modern roadway with cars that cannot run. Changing the system does not necessarily change the individual but could address factors that keep the individual inoperative or static. Stress is produced by one's response to the system. One's response is dictated by one's own make up.

Knowledge and change

Knowledge should dictate behaviour. Demanding one's own way will deprive oneself of the best. Change is related to being unstuck from old forms of doing and thinking. All worries and fears are illusions. One can get trapped in them. Change occurs as these are faced for what they are - illusions, not real, but an illusion to keep one trapped in a way of thinking and doing that keeps one paralysed. All one's memories, feelings, are now in the past, but are only an influence if one allows them to rule. Now one must live for the now and not in the past, for the past is an illusion. I cannot bring it back just as I cannot bring the dead back. So why waste my time in changing what is an illusion?

Organisations and change

All change within an organisation is because of not working towards agreed goals. The only way to manage anxiety is to move the goal posts. Decisions made at meetings need to be adhered to, and no change until the following meeting. Change needs to be followed through. Anxiety to change can only be addressed as change is followed through, and not by continuously changing. Splitting allows one's anger to be directed at a particular person or group, who are then scapegoated, and then possibly expelled with the resulting guilt. It is important to address these issues within the group; otherwise it can be destructive. Until the splitting is addressed the community will fail to be therapeutic. So also in any group splits occur, even in marriages. It is one's badness that is split off into the partner, who is then perceived as alien and attacked. Communication will prevent this and will be tackled when it occurs.

Family therapy

Family therapy can bring about a change in the way the family has handled a particular problem. This then must go on to looking at ways to meet needs more appropriately. Change of structure, provision of limits and love, leads to growth and change and integration of personality. More chaotic families need firm limits to contain negative feelings and to allow for the expression of positive feelings. More rigid families need to relax and assume responsibility for negative feelings, that is, helped to express them, and own them, as well as express positive feelings.

Systems theory

Systems theory keeps the pathology outside the individual, but fails to address the deep needs and conflicts of the individual. It is only a superficial solution to the deeper problems of man - the problem of sin and its effects. Deliverance is freeing the person from his past, which frees the person from an idealistic future [an illusion].

The larger picture

Do not be side tracked by the minutiae. Step back and see the larger picture. You need to do this every time you get stuck. You are taken up with a doctrine or one minor point, which is enlarged out of proportion to the real thing. Your emotions get tied up to keep you fixed. Take a break - see how when you do this - you unstick yourself to see the larger picture. This is so important to maintain a balance in your life. This is how a boat remains in balance otherwise it could topple over. A bird has 2 wings to keep in balance. We have 2 legs to keep in balance. It is only a plane that is in balance that can move forward to reach its destination. You need to have your life in balance - to move forward like a bullet that finds its mark. All your energy needs to flow in one direction and not be dissipated in different directions. This is where goals are able to keep you flowing in one direction. It is values that in the end give meaning and purpose and direction. Without these you will be pulled this way or the other. A divided heart will not be able to sustain the pressures, pain and trials of life.

Solutions

Solutions are the key to solving problems. That is, one should not focus on the problem but the solution to create movement. Looking at the problem and dissecting it into pieces only leads to discouragement and confusion. Looking at solutions leads to movement and optimism and hope. So in all your adventures, dilemmas, problems and predicaments focus on the solution. This is the only way forward. The system you are in will serve to keep you focused on the problem rather than the solution. Therefore you need to come up with solutions that help you break out of the system ie. a systemic problem will need a break from the systemic influences to bring about change. Only a person taking a different stance can break the habitual patterns that maintain the system. This then puts pressure on the system.

Creating difference

This difference will lead to creative solutions unless the group is too resistant to change. Therefore your position in the group to provide the difference will create others to change to find solutions when otherwise they will be stuck in their positions.

An alternative, which will threaten, moves the protagonists into action to address the crisis thus created by difference. If the protagonists don't move or find a solution then the threat is that the opposition's place will be implemented especially if the opposition is the manager who has the power to implement. This is the way to bring about change ie. create difference which then has to be addressed and a new equilibrium is found.
So also in families, work, society, problems that arise are opportunities for growth. It's only when the system fails to see problems as opportunities that it remains stuck. The players then lose heart and either give up or operate on automatic pilot and the problem controls them.
The only way problems will be seen as opportunities for growth is if the person or persons involved look to solutions. The pursuit of solutions then leads to happenings that bring about change within one's self or in the system. Systemic change will bring about a change in the pattern of relationships that will lead to the problem being solved. Paradigm shifts can also bring about change especially if the problem is the perception, thinking, feeling and behaviour of the individual. So the first step is to diagnose if the problem is a systemic one or one that is related to the coping skills or patterns of the individual. Both problem and attempted solutions sometimes reinforce each other and keep the individual and the system stuck.

Celebrate difference

One of the ways to deal with difference is to separate. The other way is to accept our differences. We can compromise in areas of difference but this is not possible if separation is part of the agenda.
The people create ambience - positive people produce a positive atmosphere.
Don't get stuck in the nitty gritty - always keep the general picture in mind. If you lose the context then you have lost the plot. Especially when investigating the source of the problem it is important to keep the larger picture in mind. It is like a

camera that focuses on the specific but loses the context if the background is not there. It is like the sore thumb that takes all the attention although it is only a part of the whole body.

Problem solving

Always let the others decide - this is a shift. When one gives the answers there will always be resistance to it, as people want to be sure - however if the answers come from someone else then there is greater possibility for implementation to take place. So the approach would be to have a balance. If one is working as a group then the group will need to be energised to come up with solutions. The solutions of the group will then enable the decisions to be implemented. If one is too controlling then the group becomes dependent and this will be okay but then the individuals in the group will not grow. Growth will occur as responsibility is delegated. Accountability then ensures that the job is done. If there is no accountability then the group will regress to a mass that never decides. So group energy needs to be capitalised but decisions have to be made and this is possible only if power is invested in one person to decide – the manager. No decision is perfect. Resistances have to be addressed. Imbalance in power is one kind of resistance. Even if it is negative power - it still has the power to resist. So address these issues and in so doing there will be release.

Asking questions

Imposing my position on others will bring a reaction. I need to ask questions that will enable the other person to look for answers and this will enable that person to feel respected and acknowledged. Leaders serve in this way. They show the lead not by feeding but by leading - getting others to find answers. This is true independence and maturity. There is no right way. Each person has his own way of looking at things. However, if a person is stuck, that is when he needs help to unstick himself. It is this process of getting them out of the rut that will lead to a new way of looking at things. Conflicts arise over control issues and therefore the strategic need to be developed is to enable individuals to choose. Choices will then lead to a situation that will enable others freely to operate in a climate of harmony. So this is the key to conflict resolution - each one decides and then looks to come to a corporate decision that will work. There is energy released in conflict that can lead to growth and maturity. Don't take on the conflicts of others but be a guide or facilitator and see how differently they will behave. You are a specialist to help people to come to their own answers. This is the way forward. Don't be too prescriptive. Yet there are families that need containment, that need to be held. This means supportive work. Others need to grow. Each one needs to be accepted for who they are; yet change is possible when people focus on change for attaining a goal.

Psychological and Spiritual insights

These insights are a combination of psychological and spiritual concepts, issues and breakthroughs.

Anger and anxiety/depression

Unexpressed anger can work itself into anxiety or depression. Sometimes there is a mixture of both anxiety and depression. When denial is the main defence mechanism then the anxiety could be converted into a physical symptom. This is why it is so important to face up to some of our thoughts and feelings directly, rather than let it fester within us. Some allow anxiety to eat away inside them. Others express it in unhelpful ways leading to violence. When anger is expressed towards others, it is because others are seen as the source of the discomfort. The effects of sin are to blind people and therefore what we see is a distortion of the real situation. We therefore respond to a distorted situation, and so our responses are likewise unhealthy.

The key to overcoming anxiety is to commit all to Jesus. When we commit our anger, anxiety, etc., to Him, then we are free to be ourselves rather than a distortion of ourselves. This is a process of healing. When we are free of the anxiety then we will be able to express ourselves freely. The Holy Spirit in us will express His image through us as we conform to His image. Every power or spirit that we conform to, or are subjected to, we will become. Trusting Christ will free us from the power of sin, which causes anxiety and helps us to express our real selves. Because we are held by love we will fear no evil. We can therefore express love, for no one will be able to hurt us since we are held by Christ's love. We are then able to give ourselves to another, which is a hallmark of love, not fearing rejection, since rejection would have no power to hurt as before.

Only when there is a sense of tension can change occur. If we always accommodate then no change will occur. Lack of discipline means spending a lot of time on weeding rather than feeding and growing.

Change

I am responsible for my actions and reactions. Over reactions are especially due to splitting ie. a part of me is split off from the rest of me. This way I am able to stand on the nice part and blame the other person for my negative reaction. Wisdom means application. Without application there is no growth. It is not trying to be loving, but being in Christ loving others and ministering to Jesus in them, which is important. It is when I loose sight of myself and see Jesus in me, that I will reflect His image and glory. Being like Christ is to live His life now, as I identify with His life in me. All difficulties and problems should be seen as opportunities for the flesh to die and to reflect Christ's image in me. When I feel unable or anxious or angry, I ask Jesus to take over, and His peace will come over me, and I am able to think clearly and deal wisely.

God's laws are for right living. When one takes responsibility for one's feelings and thoughts and stops projecting, then change will occur.

Consciousness of my sinfulness makes me humble enough to accept people as they are. Where people are accepted as they are, than peace and harmony will flow. The propensity to focus on the minutiae is because of deception and the need to prove oneself as better than others. Living to please no one but Jesus. When one is concentrating on the heart condition, then change will occur. Concentrating on the heart means changing attitudes. Changing the outside is just plasterwork to hide what is inside. Concentrating on changing the system or behavioural change is also the same. Basic change occurs only when one is able to change sinful behaviour. Splitting occurs because of the gap between the real and the false.

All those blocked up feelings need to be confronted and released so that the fears that bind one will be released, and the person set free. Anxiety and fear either makes us avoid situations or accommodate to them, but rarely to confront them. God can fill me with His fruits only when I acknowledge my own unworthiness. Unless I acknowledge me and accept me, I am always going to be defensive.

Wisdom

When one concentrates on positives, it leads to action. Concentrating on negatives leads to defence which results in reactions. Only in war do you need defence. Direct energy in expelling out, rather than defence. Once you are secure in your new identity there is less chance for these regressions to occur. When the spirit leaves, all that is left is a shell. When a church loses its soul, it loses its identity, and therefore its purpose. It is important to separate a person from one's perception of him/her. All worries and fears are an illusion. Live in the now, for the past is an illusion. Let Christ come into your consciousness, and deliver you from your past.
Wisdom is the ability to see from God's point of view. Information is power. It is the need to be in control, to exercise power over others, that leads to conflict and ill feelings. Do not treat lightly the grace and mercy of God. Jesus challenged our attitudes and therefore we need to major on change in attitudes rather than changing systems. Attitudes determine our response to the system.
Acceptance is the key to healthy relationships. Where individuals do not take responsibility for their behaviour, it will lead to splitting and scape goading. The way to beat the negativity in others, and in yourself, is to rely on the Lord to love through you. Never stop loving. Be honest in all your dealings, and the Lord will look after your finances. Worry, fear, anxiety fill up a space when one is not walking in love and the fullness of the Spirit.
Without the compassion for souls, all your ministry is like dead works. Love, give and serve. Action taken in reaction always fails to see the other's point of view. Defence will weaken you. Always love and serve and know that He is in control. Practise expressing negative feelings. Jesus came to change our attitudes to God and to others. Do not give in to the emotions that destroy, but confess them. Confessing them prevents them from controlling your life. My chief calling is to serve at all times. When I confess my negative feelings I direct them to the cross for crucifixion. Replace other voices with the voice of Jesus. Difference allows for growth. Compliance

stultifies.

Facts, knowledge and information are needed to guide you but you need wisdom to put it into effect. Without wisdom, all the knowledge you have is mere wind. It blows and is felt but it does not change anything. You need God's wisdom to change the affairs of man. So as you practise operating from your true centre in Christ, all the knowledge, learnt and supernatural, will be available to you. Then pray for wisdom to implement it. Be creative and do not get stuck in a rut. It's only when you move from your centre and operate from another centre that you loose your sense of self and become a caricature of the real person.

The Lord is in control

Solutions to problems are to do with the facts, not feelings. God's love is to be experienced. There is nothing definite in this life other than death. All mans' problems are based in this- false self created in defence through life's experiences. It is only truth and love that will be able to overcome the untruth of the years. The real self operates in love and truth. Identification is the unconscious motivation that explains some present-day behaviour and transmission of patterns. The Lord is in control. Put your faith and trust in this one thing and you will succeed. It is only identification with Christ in His death, resurrection and ascension that can free us from the flesh, world and the devil. Major on affective communication- block in this area leads to difficulties in relationships. God does His work by His Spirit through the prayers of His people. When communication is halted or distorted at a feeling level it will affect relationships and lead to defensiveness and distorted perceptions. Learn how to release the resources in heaven by giving as the Spirit leads.

Living each day to the fullest- this is the will and design for each child of God. God has given you life to live each day to the glory of His Name. He is the one who gives you life and health and as you trust in Him you will be made stronger each day. All the things that hold on to you will leave you as you trust the Father of lights to shine in and through you. Purpose in your heart to serve only Him, for in this way you will be able to discern good from evil. He is your righteousness. In Him you have all things to live a victorious life. Do not go after the things that cause you to be stimulated only in your senses but desire the deeper things of the Spirit. His Spirit is in you to fill you. His blood cleanses you as you turn from all evil intentions of the heart. Be humble and seek to serve all men for in this way you will seek to please Him and draw many into His kingdom. Men seek to compare themselves with others but you must seek to please Him and not men. His Kingdom is not of this world so why seek for the pleasures and honours in this world? God is the one who will bless you and anoint you- so look to Him for all the resources you need each day.

As I operate from my true centre and concentrate on being in His presence I will operate in power and grow in strength in His grace and image. This is the only way to deliver myself from the power of my dis-eased attitudes and feelings. I don't look to others to fulfil my needs but I look to Him who is my Father in heaven to nourish me, comfort me and instruct me in the way. As I do this daily I come into my own and will be known and know what it means to be me. I am accepted and out of my strong identity in Him I will operate to overcome all my enemies. I live only to the praise of His name. I don't live to please myself but to please Him. I will be a vessel of His making- filled with His love and joy and will transmit this to others as they come in contact with me. I will not look to others to meet my needs nor will I manipulate others to meet my needs, for I know this will lead only to suffering and hurt. Rather I will direct all my needs to Him who is able to meet all my needs. I will not listen to the other voices but I shall look to Him. I will direct these other voices to Him who is able to deal with them. I shall not rationalise or excuse my thoughts and intentions and feelings but direct them all to the Cross to be crossed out so that I may be delivered from their power over me.

Voices of the past

It's the images and voices of the past that harangue you and distort the present and cause fears for the future. Remember your enemies are just vain imaginations of the flesh. They have no power over you unless you give them power. See them as challenges to overcome. For it is in the process of overcoming these pressures that you become strong. So do not give up but be bold knowing that He is with you. Yes, He will cause you to hate evil with all your heart that you will seek Him only. As you take up your position in Him and operate from your true centre then you will see all your enemies become your footstool.

Do all things in love and for the glory of His Name. Give freely and do not think in terms of returns. It's the Lord who blesses and therefore be content with what you have. Think in abundance and enlarge your heart for it is as you enlarge your heart that the Lord will be able to fill it. He will fill it with good things, love, peace, and joy and as He fills you, you will be able to share out of your abundance. The Lord does not wish you to share out of your poverty (self). God supplies the resources for His work. It's when men choose to do God's work in their own strength that it leads to worry, poverty and failure. In His strength there is no failure - only success. So be filled with Him. Do not be threatened by the negativity in this world. Give it or direct it to Him and see how He will turn it into positives through His Cross. This is what Jesus did. He came into the negative forces in this world and through His death He conquered the power of sin and triumphed in resurrection power. So also you can overcome now through faith in His finished work to triumph in every situation. Do this through faith in His finished work rather than in your own wisdom and knowledge. Bind the evil one in all his works around you and in others. By this you are binding the hands of the evil one to sow discord and invoke His peace and love wherever you are. As long as you are walking in the fullness of His Spirit, all you think, do and say will be blessed. Your life will be blessed and others will be blessed through you.

There is nothing absolute in this world. In God only is there absolute truth - for He is the Truth and He cannot lie. So put your faith and trust in Him and see how He will abundantly bless. Do not waste your energy in building yourself up.

Rather be eager to point others to Christ who is the only one other's should see in you and believe and be saved. He has not come to condemn but to save.

Imprisoned by our past

Fallen mankind seeks to be affirmed through comparison with others. They look to the creature rather than the Creator. Subjection to others is a trap in itself for one is bent towards the creature. True submission is where one is submitted to God and through this to others. Submission to others without a submission to God leads only to dependency and control by others. This is the trap that all mankind is in. First prison is of one's parents who keep us obliged to them rather than allowing us to be free to be ourselves. This is then replayed in other relationships, where, as a bound person, one replays the perceived roles of past relationships. In this way every one is bound to a certain extent and it is through the healing process that one is released from the domination of these respective roles.
In Christ, one is brought to a place of complete submission to Him who then begins the process of change and healing as one is delivered from one's past relationships and made whole in relationship with Him. The primary relationship is with Him- the Father, through Jesus Christ. This primary relationship with the Father restores one's relationships from all their neurotic longings and delivers us. This then frees us to love and relate with others from a place of security rather than insecurity.

Deprive old patterns of attention

You receive your strength and nourishment from Christ. You are the branch so you will exhibit the characteristics of Christ. Do not be taken up with the characteristics of your earthly parent. Now you belong to the vine, your heavenly Father, and the life of Jesus is in you through the Holy Spirit who lives in you. You need to move in this, your new identity. It is the regressions to the flesh that keep you bound to old fleshly ways of thinking and feeling. These will slowly lose their grip on you as you operate by faith in the new life in you. This is why it is so important to listen to the words of Christ. His Words spoken out in faith will replace those old patterns of thought, leading you to live in new ways. So be earnest in all you do and think. These patterns tend to stick to you like leeches. Do not feed these leeches by giving attention to them. Rather deprive them of attention by concentrating on Christ in you. In this way they will die as the power of God's Word strikes them and banishes them from your life.

Praise God that you now live in the resurrection power of Christ. Be on guard. For it's your thoughts that will fire up those old attitudes that will stir up the flesh into action. Give no room to them. Confess them and bring them out into the open where they can be exposed to the light and dealt a heavy blow by the Spirit who is in you to help you to fight your enemies to the end. Pray and release yourself from these old patterns of thinking and doing. He is your source of all wisdom and knowledge. Judge all things in the light of His Word and see how you will grow in knowledge and wisdom till you are able to stand against all these rulers and principalities of this dark world.

Changing old patterns

Old patterns can be broken only with concerted work to demolish them and to replace them with the new - relationship patterns, thinking patterns, actions, habits etc. First of all identify these patterns - then work on changing them - visualise them being erased from your memory and replaced with new patterns. Then practice the new patterns over and over again. You find that you remember only those things that are habits. This is possible because God is in the game of change and sanctification. He sanctifies you. God is able - trust Him. Do not let your past or present determine your future. Always believe and trust Him for the future. The future is not yet. Therefore you can trust Him to give you something new. Remember what each failure has meant - new learning, new confidence.

Never mind what others think, you do your part. This is to sail with the wind. Yet God is in the wind. It is not sailing without direction. It is to sail with your rudder, fixed on the goal ahead. This is easy when you know what the goal is. Then you work to master the hurdles or blockages to achieve the goal and you come home. Each one has his or her hurdles to master. You have given your life over to God - now trust Him to overcome through you. He won't do it for you. You have to do it with His help. You cannot overcome hurdles without doing your part. An athlete has to practice and master his body to do what it should and not what it wants. So you too must make the choices daily in order to achieve the goal.

Issues

Concentrate on issues rather than on changing the person. Acknowledge feelings - name them and spew them out. Let every difference be seen as a challenge to creativity and not a threat. Love is unconditional. Placing the Lord first frees one from self-centeredness to Christ-centeredness. One's soul is washed in the blood of Jesus. Be fair, true and faithful in your responses. Fantasies are based on feelings and not facts. Living by faith is to live in Christ and face each situation as it comes up. I don't need to be perfect- I need to be human. Being flexible is to be real with my thoughts and feelings. I must stop dealing with them in fantasy and bring them out into the light. It is not what I have, but what I am that counts. Trust and obey.

Concentrate on issues and not personalities. It is not the decision but the process that is important. It is only the fear of God that can dispel the fear of man. Never react to a negative spirit, but bind it. Always measure yourself by God's standards and not man's standards. Practise love and holiness. Knowing what you are, and who you are and the authority you have in Christ. Invoke His presence and the devil will flee. Relationship is more than doing things for each other. The missing element is the need to connect. This connection occurs when two people trust and respect each other. It is a communication of feelings and thoughts- a state of being with one another. As you are true to yourself, then you will be able to see others clearly. Concentrate on being and not doing.

Whole body filling

On the day of Pentecost, the whole body was filled- not just individuals, so it is today. The whole body has to be filled if the Church is to grow and be strong. The worldly spirit emphasises individualism. God's power is positive. Just as a product cannot be judged by what is seen, so also a person cannot be judged by what is seen. My soul has been deprived because of having to put up a front. The Lion of Judah lives in me. Your defensiveness is an indicator of your self-centeredness. Introspection leads to defensiveness. Practice His presence. Order and creativity needs to go hand in hand for balanced living. Train your mind to live in the now in Jesus. Worry strengthens the flesh and weakens the spirit. Evil is to be resisted. Compromise is the talk and thinking of the world. Practicing His Presence means dying to self and living in Christ. God is concerned about how well you have loved and obeyed Him. No compromise. God and you are a majority.

Secrets

Humility is to be stripped of these defences and to live in His presence. Secretiveness is the cause of a lot of illness. Vain imaginations cause defensiveness and withdrawal - cast them down and direct them to the cross of Jesus. Nothing is certain in this world except death. I can either be real with myself and walk in the positive fear of God, or in the negative fear of the other. Be submissive, teachable and a servant to all. It is through trials and tribulations that your faith will be tested and purified and made strong. Not I, but Christ. Humility is practicing the presence of Jesus. A true test of a man is by his reactions. God will judge me according to how much I have loved. Look for the best way and not for one's own way. Identify with the pain of others, for in this way you set others free and also it is easier to listen to the other. Christ's way is "no rights"- all you deserve is death.

Christ is the judge. Serving Christ in the other. Try and put yourself in the position of the other and you will not be defensive and react. Only Christ should control me. Faith is the realisation of things hoped for, the proof of things not seen. Stiff upper lip is the product of emotional frozenness.

Rationality at the expense of emotional freedom. You must maintain the position of death so that others do not influence you, but Christ in you. By faith. you maintain this position moment by moment. Love the sinner but hate his actions. Have a holy hatred against all sinful feelings, thoughts and behaviour. I look to the Cross, my only hope of salvation. Look up and imagine the Cross and let all negative feelings and thoughts be directed to the Cross of Christ. To appreciate others it is important to identify with them and their situation. Death to self means "no rights", so that Christ has all rights.

Independence and serving one another

Independence only seems to cater to man's selfish desire to be in control and to serve self. In the process others may benefit but the motivating force is self. This is opposed to the kingdom of God. Not I but Christ is the theme of the Kingdom of God. Serving, giving and loving is the way of the Kingdom. All your energy is not spent in how to gain for yourself but for others. It's the change of attitude- always being last and not first. Always seeking to bless and not to be blessed. Always seeking to serve and not to be served. Always giving and not seeking to take.

The world without God seeks to serve self and to make it secure. This is an illusion. One finds oneself only in another. For a Christian, one finds oneself in God and in the service of others.

Renouncing, repentance, forgiveness and faith in the finished work of Christ on the Cross is the way to free yourself. Live in the now and feel and be as you think and feel inspired by the Holy Spirit in you. You need fight only against the devil and his comrades. In love you don't have to fight but to flow with

Him as He leads you.

Feelings

For one who has operated in a defensive mode to protect oneself from the negative feelings, one needs to tap into Christ's love, which never changes. Fixed in Him one is able to allow oneself to be vulnerable. This characteristic is important. Do not allow another to dump their feelings on you. Always remember it's their feelings in reaction or otherwise. Separate their feelings from yours. Each one must take responsibility for their own feelings. Do not try and ignore or defend your own feelings for when you do then you deny yourself and in the process, hate yourself. This is what leads to poor self-esteem. Your fear of acknowledging your negative feelings then leads to it directing itself against you. Feelings are feelings and when one takes responsibility for them then they will not be directed at others but will be owned by one self. This ownership then allows one to express it without fear of being blamed or causing guilt in others.
When feelings take control, it's because you have allowed yourself to be ruled by them. Feelings have power only when they are either feared or denied. What is not confronted always is given power. This is why secrets have got such a hold on people's lives. So be open and do not hold on to information or thoughts or feelings. For what is held on to will control your life. Be prepared to be a fool but be yourself. Don't support the pretence of what you are not. This is deception of the highest kind. There will always be fear associated with such projections. Instead, be open and vulnerable.

Coming in touch with one's feelings

I need to do my part in keeping myself clear of all defensive behaviours. This will enable me to come in touch with my own feelings. This then will enable me to touch others and separate my feelings from others. It is so easy to work through ones own feelings through the experience of another. It is more painful to work through ones own feelings - for these leads to threat and loss. Once one comes in touch with ones feelings - the defence goes and one is no longer threatened or controlled by these feelings. To enable you to come to this place you must accept yourself as you are in Christ and then walk the straight and narrow road to liberty. So be strong. Let the barrier down. Come present to yourself. Take responsibility for your feelings and behaviour. Changes occur as you do so. Don't blame others - rather see how you can change or be the solution or part of it.

Knowledge is held in your mind to be accessed for the understanding and application to life situations. Some of this knowledge is learned through academic pursuits and others through life experiences. It's knowledge that leads to experiencing life in a new way that leads to abundant life. The source of knowledge is as important as the knowledge itself. This is why it is important to be critical of all knowledge. Knowledge educates your mind to see things in a new light. There are three types of knowledge. The purely physical knowledge informs one of what can be seen and touched.

These can be learnt from observation. Such knowledge is easily gained from books. Then there is knowledge of relationships and behaviour. This is usually learnt through life experiences through relationships. This cannot be learnt just through reading. The study of this kind of knowledge has to be gained through involvement with others. Such knowledge cannot be gained in a laboratory. Thirdly knowledge from the spiritual realm comes through a divine encounter. All three influences affect an individual. Ignorance or blindness in one affects the other two areas. A person is only whole when he is in tune in all three areas. The knowledge of God is the highest form of knowledge for it envelops the other two. A man who is in tune with God will be in tune in the other two areas. It's important therefore to be moving in all three areas and to be discovering in all three areas. So do not be side tracked by being pushed into one area of investigation when you know that the whole is greater than the sum of the parts.

of man is limited

's knowledge is limited within the system of investigation. God's knowledge is eternal and is not limited by any particular system. It encompasses all things. Therefore judge all things in the light of His wisdom and knowledge. Do not be sidetracked by pieces of evidence but try and see the whole picture. God's light shines on the pathology and delivers the answers. So do not get stuck in pathology but look and listen for God's word-knowledge and wisdom in the situation that will remove the pathology or ways of thinking and doing. In this way you not only free the individual but also the system.

An introspective approach does not look outward to solutions but inwards to problems. This is a way of looking and thinking that takes one deeper into the problem rather than out of it. God's way is always to take us out of the mess we are in rather than deeper into it.

Therefore be careful that you do not get trapped or sucked into the systems of the world. Listen and learn but always look for solutions and not pathology. This will free you from the system you are in. Thinking in terms of pathology maintains the system, which is pathological. Pathological thinking will not lead to solutions. Only one who is whole can lead others to wholeness.

Belief systems

The basis of all thought and perception is based on belief systems. If your belief system is ordered by some popular theory then that is what you will see. So also when God enters your life, His light in you will guide your perceptions. So let His light shine brighter as you acknowledge His presence within you.

Individuals bring their own thoughts and feelings into a situation. These perceptions are their own and have to be challenged. When not challenged then they will believe that they are right. People get stuck in the ways they think and do things. It's only conflict and challenge that will cause a reappraisal of the familiar ways of doing things. Theories abound but what is true is only seen by its fruit. This is why theories can educate but will have no benefit till it is tested and received and if it is true will produce fruit of its kind. Even theories need faith to produce fruit. Whatever is man made can only be proved through application. No amount of theorising can produce the goods unless it is applied. If applied and nothing happens then the theory is disproved.

So be sure as to what you are applying. All psychology is rooted in self. It's roots are sinful although some of the applications may be sound. It is not rooted on the basis of good or evil but good and evil. Because of this all its findings are not absolute. Pure science is yes or no, not both. Either a drug has effects or not. Therefore it is important to test each approach, however effective it may be, on the principles revealed by the Word of God. Any scientific method or result must be based on empirical evidence. Proving a theoretical approach by personal experience is as good as practicing witchcraft. Anyone can practice what he thinks is good but is open to lead people into bondage rather than freedom.

All knowledge needs to be based on fact not just opinions. What is based on fact is proven through research and experimentation. But there is a bit of knowledge that is experience based. Beliefs are a powerful source of knowledge for they are based on personal emotional attachment - this means that it is close to the heart and mind of the person - engraved in his soul and a source of his identity, self, meaning. Without this the person is just a collection of cells, facts, knowledge with no meaning. Belief is what gives meaning - this is what differentiates man from other animals. Belief in God, in oneself, in a system, in others, in a venture, project, and mission is what provides the purpose to achieve the goal - the driving force. So the why - meaning, is what drives one to find the means to achieve the goal. To be financially free for what purpose - to be free to do what I have always wanted to do - to love, serve, learn and leave a legacy. To be able to branch out in different areas not be caged in by fear of what the other person will do but to know that I will be able to stand on my own, to be able to contribute fully to others and help others to stand on their own. This freedom can lead to pride and selfishness or to an entrepreneurial, giving, serving and helping spirit that seeks to serve others. True freedom is from within. Money cannot totally set a person free. Loneliness and isolation are evils that cannot be filled with money and things. It is to love and be loved - and this comes through service. I choose to serve that others may be rich.

Belief in anything will produce the results of the object believed in. If you believe in T.M. or hypnosis, then your trust in the effectiveness of it will bring you the required relief. So also trust in God. A man is able to do any thing because he has the capacity to use his imagination. Now what is believed is important. The source of what one receives binds one to the spirit of that belief system. This is why one needs to discern what one believes. Your trust in the Lord enables you to keep yourself pure because His blood cleanses you and keeps you free from the impurities of the flesh and of this world.

Belief in any system makes you a victim of that system. The family is a very powerful system. The parents create the system, which is pathological or functional. The children are the victims of the system. They may react to the system and get out of it or be scapegoated by the system and be ejected. Parents themselves are victims of their own family belief system.

These beliefs, whether good or bad, keep the individuals and the system together (bound). It's the power of these beliefs that keep individuals bound to the system. The individuals within this system will not be freed from the grip of their beliefs till they are identified, named and renounced. A system in distress gives rise to symptoms. Addressing the symptoms does not address the pathological system.

However, within the system, individuals carry disorders that maintain the system in its dysfunctional form. This is why some individuals escape while others are trapped and all the negativity and problems are encapsulated in this one individual who serves as the family's dustbin for their badness. The rest of the family can blame or excuse their own responsibility because of this one sick member.

In Christ, all other beliefs will have to bow to His Name. So do not entertain other gods (belief systems) that are contrary to His ways. Entrust yourself completely into His hands. He is sufficient for you. Trust Him completely. Let His death on the Cross be always before you. Let His resurrection life give you hope for the gifts and fruits to be expressed through His Spirit in you.

Unity in one's belief system

If one needs to reach the highest potential - one needs to be united in ones belief system. The whole body, mind and spirit must believe. It is this belief that will then energise the subconscious to produce that, which is beyond consciousness. That is why meditation and faith is able to tap resources beyond the conscious self. Within one there is a reservoir of unconscious forces that seek to destroy or waste. Energy that is forced against oneself will destroy. Energy in synergy will create something above what is expected. Expectation is high when there is synergy. So it is your belief in what you want that leads you to achieve. Lack of belief will work against you. So you need to be sure that what you are thinking, feeling and doing are in unity. If there is disharmony, the conflict within will sap your energy and vitality. His blood washes and cleanses you as you repent of the evil and there is release from the sin and harmony is established. The spirit, soul and body need to work in harmony. Where there is disharmony there will be a sapping of energy. So be careful how you operate. If you want to achieve beyond yourself then you must go deeper into yourself - into the vital core of yourself to bring forth the true potential. Fear and anxiety and inner conflict only dissipate your energy. That is why it is good to look outward. Looking inward only leads to regression. Looking outward gives you the ability to change. Then all your energy is directed towards problem solving. If one is in defence then all the energy is taken up in serving self. In Christ, you have died to the old man - no need to defend him. You are in Christ as a new creation. So now you are filled in the Holy Spirit. The Holy Spirit will lead you and guide you. The pull of the flesh is still there but as you take up your cross daily, you die to the old man and he becomes weaker. This is sanctification. This then leads to a bolder self - increased faith in God - reliance on Him and to operate in faith, believing in the best. Yes, I will not control - I will love, for love heals, forgives, gives and looks to build others - not to compete but to share. This is how one can grow. I am dead - Christ lives in me. I need to allow these beliefs to so sink in me and do the work of regeneration. People who have been filled are so full of God that they can expect the impossible. This is what faith in God achieves.

Emptiness

The need to put up a front and to invest in a front is because of emptiness within. The front you can see and therefore feel important or useful but there is no depth to this life. Therefore do not be taken up with the outward but invest in the inward. The outward is just a front to cover up what is not seen in the inward. When a man is at rest and at peace in the inside then it is reflected on the outside. A man who operates by denial is unaware of his inward state. He operates in the outward and deceives himself by thinking he is alright when he is not. The spirit of this world operates on the outward man. The lusts of the eyes are his area of operation to deceive others by what they see. Do not be deceived. All men are sinners. They grope in darkness and look to outward systems to keep them going on. But these outside props will one day collapse for all that is made is prone to destruction or decay. Only that which is created has eternal life. Now this life is in Jesus. Man lost his capacity to have eternal life through the fall. Jesus has come that man may have eternal life. This life is in the Son. The devil will deceive man through replicas of the real. The pride of life will keep man working out his salvation in his own strength. Not all man's endeavours are bad or evil. Look for the good in all things. So do not be deceived.

Being one

God sees you as one. You may see yourself as made up of

parts. It's when you see yourself as one that you become one and operate as one. The one way to become one is to see yourself from God's position. He is three in one yet He is one. You too are three in one and need to see this otherwise you will see only in part.

In Him, as you abide in Him and live in Him, you become one. You operate from His centre in you and therefore you operate as a new creature. It's when you operate from your position in Christ that you will feel one and not be overwhelmed through conflict of the different parts of you. It's when one part is attended to more than the other that conflict comes. But in Christ, there will be balance. So abide in Him and see how His Spirit in you will bring you to a place of unity. So also in the body of Christ, it is when each is united in the Spirit that true unity will occur.

United in Him we become one. All things move together in harmony. Conflict is a sign of disharmony and the need to return to your true centre. God in you leads you as you walk in His ways and remain centred in Him.

Introspection

Introspection is a disease that kills the soul. Christ's answer to this disease is crucifixion and receiving His new life. Trying to change this way of thinking and living by another form of introspective activity (like dynamic psychotherapy) is to make the sin more sophisticated and acceptable. This is not cure but like dressing to a picture that is ugly. You can never dress up sin. This is rationalisation. Sin needs to be confronted like any other evil. It needs to be bound and renounced. It needs to be seen as an evil that should not be entertained but cursed. Evil if given a chance will have a hold on you. Sin if entertained will have a hold on you. That's why it needs to be bound in Jesus name. Then it cannot influence you. Then it needs to be confessed and repented of so that you can be freed from its power. Now you have the power of God to do good and not get entangled in ceaseless, unproductive, introspective activity. One is man's way, the other is trusting God to deliver and set free.

Roles

Roles restrict an individual to perform within that perceived position and therefore elicits certain reactions and perceptions from others. Doctor is perceived as intelligent, know-it-all, upper class, sophisticated, etc. A person is straitjacketed by the expectations of others in this role. Therefore, when a person is stripped of this familiar role, then he operates as if without an identity. This affects his thought processes and feelings. Some individuals are so role-oriented that they feel confused and lost when operating beside their role.
This is why it is so important to always think of the person behind the role. The role is to fulfil a function. The person is always there and has needs like any other human being. It's to this person that Jesus comes to minister. However, one's role sometimes is a barrier to one receiving ministry. The pride that goes with the role keeps a person from receiving. This is why a person must come to Jesus with a need. Without a need there is no need for a Saviour. The secure and unneeded are blinded by the god of this world. Like a house that stands with all its grandeur, so is a person who invests all in his role or possessions. One day, it will all be burned down. What is left? It is the soul that lives forever.
So also too much knowledge puffs up. Its love and the service to others that counts. Many in this world suffer because of others. In this world difference is created only because of the greed of man. All are the same in God's sight because all have sinned. There is no one better. You are saved by grace through faith. There is nothing you can do but rest in this fact.
So also beware of being deluded or deceived into a false sense of security. This is never real. The only real security is to know that you belong to the Father and that you are known by Him. This revelation will put all other things in perspective. All the lusts of the flesh, the pride of life will so disgust and horrify you. Oh, the sinfulness of my own heart. Who can stand in the sight of a holy God?

Thoughts

All that you think is just that thoughts. However these thoughts have an influence on your life. The influence is to do with attitudes, feelings and actions. So beware of your thoughts. Sometimes you feel things that are lustful and sinful. Where do they come from? From the pit. The devil in his crafty way is always out to put you down. So listen to God's voice in you. You have the responsibility to check those thoughts and feelings. You are the gatekeeper. Now see how good a gatekeeper you are. Ask the Holy Spirit to guard the gate to your heart and soul for then what happens is when the devil comes knocking, he will be faced with the Cross and the blood. No evil can enter the door of your heart and mind that is covered with His blood. So check your heart and soul. Every feeling of negativity needs to be directed to the Cross and cleansed. It's in this way slowly, little by little, that the land will be regained. The Holy Spirit will do it as you set your will to work with Him.

Dealing with negative thoughts

Without faith one cannot please God and know God. How important it is not to judge others. Lord, forgive me. How one cannot stop the way other's think - it is important to respect others the way they are - to concentrate on the positives - to encourage the positives in others rather than looking for the negatives. It is so important to empty one self of all negativity. It is the negatives that sap me of my strength. Just as Samson's strength was dependent on his hair - so my strength is dependent on my faith in God. Faith removes all negativity - faith is anti doubt. Then in this resourceful state I can overcome all things. I need therefore to be watchful and each day be energised to conquer - to press on - till the mountains are razed to the ground.

Theories and theories

Do not be intimidated by all the psychobabble that goes on in your midst. This is all the work of untruth in your midst. You need to continue to work in truth overcoming untruth through the truth of God's word. People choose to understand in different ways. There are different epistemological approaches that try and sell or understand behaviour through man made theories. Beware of these approaches. It's like brain washing. It's got some truth in it but most of it has its roots in the pit. Select that which makes sense. Most of it is for the defence of the therapist then for the sake of change for the patient. No change can come about till the fact of sin can be faced. Any truth that excludes God is from the pit. The devil will bring these approaches to popularity for they are self centred and only cater to the flesh. You need to rise above these theories and practices. Language does bind a group of people together although it may do no good to anyone. Many are bound together by such untruth all over the world.

Faith in Jesus Christ

God's truth working through love and faith is the only way forward. Change is possible to anyone who believes. So it is not systems or theories or techniques but faith in Jesus Christ working through love that can change the world. Everyday man can come up with a new approach but God's Word will last forever. He is the only one who is alive. When you look at your own life you can recognise how puny it is. Do not hold on to it. Let go and let God fill you with His Word of truth. Put your faith in God's Word. Then the power of His Word will be released in you. This power will so influence your body, mind and spirit that you will be released from the untruth that has been sown into your life.

In one realm you work to earn a living. On another realm you work to be loved and to love. And on the third and upper realm you operate to work out your faith in God. All this is possible as God has control over your life. It's only a man who wants to hold on to what he has that needs to fear. If all has been given to God then He can be trusted to look after what He has given to you. This is faith. The devil cannot rob you of what you have given to God for God is the Keeper. But the devil can rob you of what you have, for he is out to destroy you.

Defences

The defences of the flesh keep one bound and not free. The defences are there to serve self. Why need defences if you are free? You are guilty, that's why you need defences. Your defences keep you blind to the fears and anxieties within. The only way out is Christ. He will come and take all your burdens-anxieties, fear and worries and pain and loneliness and replace them with His love, joy and peace. For this, you don't need defences. You only need defences to keep hatred and unlove in.

Children and defences

A child is less defensive and shows his/her true characteristics by acting out what he feels inside. His defences are not strong to keep all those fears and hatred inside and therefore it spills out. What the child needs is security to know that the adults around him will keep him safe. If they can't by their own reactions to him then he will realise his worst fears and finally be rejected and abandoned. Some children escape into fantasy to continue to cope in a world where they have felt abandoned. They don't feel anymore, for to feel, is to fear, is to suffer loss, abandonment and rejection.

Defensiveness

Defensiveness leads to a loss of feelings. What is defended against is the feeling - fear, anger, resentment - it is a cover up. The deeper feelings are covered up by a superficial friendliness. This is what leads to a distortion in reality. The feelings distort reality so that one can function in the edited version of reality. The perception of reality based on a distortion due to defensive operations leads to lying to ourselves and to others. We therefore relate to others and ourselves in fantasy. There isn't a reality base. It is difficult to come in touch with our feelings or that of others. This then leads to misunderstandings and conflicts. The only way through this is to strip ourselves of these defences and trust ourselves to Christ. He then enables us to feel the pain of being human. Defences are to protect us from the pain. When the pain gets too much and there is a breakdown in defences - this leads to violence or self-harm leading to depression. These are the fears of the unknown - therefore we keep operating in the way we are familiar in. This does not enable us to change. Our defensive position controls us and others to conform to us. This then leads to isolation and the fear of abandonment. A crisis then occurs and either the defences drop and change occurs or a breakdown occurs. Reaching rock bottom is to reach a place of rest. For from this place, one can build upwards. Fearing reaching rock bottom is to fear the unknown. From this place one does not need to react to defensive behaviour anymore. One can be oneself. Failure has the same effect. Look for the positive in every negative experience. Sometimes a very negative experience helps us to appreciate our blessings. Look for the opposite. Be humbled in success. This way you keep yourself in balance. Words are good but it is the personal application that results in life. It is the doing that makes me feel alive. Isolation and one upmanship do not lead to life - it leads to loneliness. One needs to be open with ones thoughts and feelings. If you live by saying what the other person needs to hear then you live and die without knowing yourself. It is living by ones own standards that exercise a higher standard. Living in this way challenges you and others. You learn to accept others for what they are when you accept yourself as you are.

Freedom in Christ

Your defences keep you from experiencing your fears. But Christ has come to assure you of His love. That He has taken all your fears. Now you can live in His love-fearless. Come to Him and abide in Him. Realising His love for you, you cannot but express it in so many ways. That's why praise is so vital to the life of the spirit. Praise recognises the work that Christ has done. So you can praise Him at all times-in sickness and health, in abundance and poverty-for the riches of the kingdom are in you and nothing can rob you of these.

So rejoice and be glad. Shout out your gladness and rejoice in His riches in you. Christ has come to refresh you and to anoint you. So give all to Him and live each day to the glory of His name. He is your Father and you are His son. Rejoice in Him always and be glad. Let His praises fill you. Live freely, for you have freely received. Owe man nothing but to love to the end.

Relationships

Beware of those thoughts and feelings that are stirred up through relationships. They are there to show you how proud and self-sufficient you are.

God's way is truth and love. His way is full of love, joy and peace. Where these abound you can be sure that His Spirit is present. So do not judge by the outward but in confidence trust in God whatever the circumstances. God knows what is best. Remember Job lost everything but he still trusted in God. So do not allow your circumstances, thoughts and feelings to determine your responses. Your responses must now change, as you trust in God and Jesus whom He has sent. The devil will try and deceive you to believe otherwise but God is in control. You have committed your life to Him so you can trust Him to lead and to guide. Practise this in all areas of your life. Rely on Him to impart His love, knowledge and wisdom. Do not go back to past ways of doing things for they are self-centred and sinful. Have this mind in you of trusting God at all times. Don't be driven by ambition and all the other ways of doing things. Trust in Him for He is the one who marks you as present.

Self centred life style

Change occurs as I surrender all to Him and trust Him to do the work of changing me. I cannot change myself as I am trapped in my own ways of thinking and believing. I am stuck in my own rut. I need another to show me the way out of my rut. I trust in the objective real to show me as I sit back and see His divine finger plotting the course of my life. He has predestined the way I will go. Now I need to follow His plan for my life. It is not what I do but how I do it and for whom. I can either do it for my own glory in my own strength or for His glory in His strength. This is the difference between life and death. A man can find himself only in another. Too much concentration on self leads to a strengthening of oneself that leads to a narcissistic life style- a satisfaction in ones own beliefs and ways. This may sound very nice and whole but is still very self centred. Self-centred people are deceived in thinking that they are alright. It's only in a crisis that the true self is revealed. All the make up of self is to invest in the outward, which will not stand on the day of reckoning.

God builds from the inside- man builds from the outside. What is built from the outside is sensed through the senses. What is built from the inside is spiritually sensed. This means that one needs to be spiritually attuned to the realm of the spiritual. This is possible for all men for all were created spiritual. However the source of the spiritual determines where a man will go.

There are 2 gods in this world- the Almighty God and his foe- Satan. They both influence the world. God's righteous servants are influenced through His Spirit. Satan's servants are influenced through demons. This is only taught as a realm in Christian theology although the presence of good and evil are present in all teachings. However the source is not differentiated as in persons. God in Christian theology is a person as Satan is. Therefore a Christian can have a personal relationship with God revealed through His Son Jesus.

Religions of the world

The isms of this world will teach that all religions are the same and that all believe in God and seek God. Christianity teaches otherwise. There is only one way. Beware of the forces that would deceive. It is more acceptable to preach that all roads lead to Rome. However God's Word cannot be changed by mans word. God's Word will stand the test of time. Man will try to water down God's Word. But man will not threaten God. You have one life. You have a choice as to how you are going to live this life. Your choice will determine how your walk in this life will be like. There is no other way to come to God the Father then through His Son Jesus. So choose to follow Him. He is your righteousness. Do not be threatened by the influences of the world or isms that promise a salvation that is not the gospel way.

Sanctification

True self-acceptance is only possible in Christ. Why? Because it is only in Christ that I am free (cleansed in His blood) to accept my new self. The old self is crucified in Christ. The new self in Christ is being renewed. It has not been totally delivered ie. although I am whole in Christ, I am being sanctified to be like Christ. Christ has finished that work on Calvary but I have to walk in it daily and be renewed daily. This is an area that is confused with the old self, which is selfish and self-centred.
Psychology does not recognise the old self (self cut off from God through the fall and turned into itself). This is the spiritual self - the Adamic nature. This part can never be changed. However everyone has a soul. This soul is in Christ, being sanctified. The Christian is free to be for he does not now need to contend with his old self, which is crucified. However he has to contend with his psychological self, which is being renewed. Both for the Christian and non- Christian, this is the area where healing can occur in Christ and otherwise. It is not changing the old nature but the part of us that has been torn, hurt, rejected, through all the negative influences-spiritual, emotional and relational. The discoveries in psychology enable one to understand the operation of the "psychological self". Many are trapped through lies and truth needs to be spoken for relief. Self-acceptance in this area is the acceptance of the person who you and I are. Self-rejection is the opposite. Self-acceptance is the mature position of a Christian and non-Christian. Both have battles in this area.

The Christian can fight through his knowledge of his acceptance in Christ. A non-Christian seeks other ways to meet this need.

Old self and self

Man created in God's image has the ability to discover the laws of God that are universal. These principles apply to all, just as the rain falls on the wicked and righteous. So also there are principles that govern our emotional lives. If these are rejected then the Church suffers a loss. Just as man has a physical being which suffers and responds to treatment so also the psychological self.

Self-esteem is a fruit of self-acceptance. This is not a denial of self but a self that feels good also loves and shares and gives freely. So this is not a support for the old self but that part of our being that constitutes our emotional make-up. We all need healing and deliverance in this area. A Christian who is able to accept himself in Christ is on the road to healing. However many Christians don't, for they confuse the old man with the true self. It is unfortunate that the term self is used in both areas. It is the separation of the two selves that will enable us to appreciate the difference and not reject truth that is vital and healthy for all to know. This is the area of battle.

When you are filled and led by the Holy Spirit, then you are no more under the influence of this world or its ways. The new way you walk will both attract and repel the world. However, Jesus has shown us His way-way of love and freedom from the systems of this world. It's only a man who knows God personally can rely on Him to show him the way, step by step. This is the walk of faith, trusting God and walking in obedience to Him. The moment you give in to another, you are under their control. Only God should control your life. It's the fear of others influence or favour that leads to your being crippled. Now step out in faith from these prison walls and walk in the heavenlies. You are now open to other influences of the spirit world. This world cages you and keeps you bound to its ways of thinking and doing. When you operate in the realm of the Spirit, you are no more bound but free. So come and be free. No more bound but free. This is the gospel. Man however has bound the gospel by man made doctrines and laws and traditions. God has only two doctrines - love God; love man. If these two can be fulfilled, then you are in the right path. However, because man needs rules, he has crippled himself.

Interdependency

In His presence you live the crucified life. In Him alone you operate in victory. You are to be the salt and the light. Don't react - for that is of the flesh. Rather think at how you can be part of the solution. When you react then you become part of the problem. So be proactive. Proactivity is the strategy of the visionary. Proactivity keeps you from being reactive. Proactive thinking enables you to think and plan ahead. Reactive thinking is defensive thinking. So do not be caught up in this. Reactive people are always defensive and in a position of dependence and disempowered. Therefore the strategy of empowering others makes them proactive and independent. This independence then leads to encouraging others to be independent, empowered and this process creates a situation of inter dependency which is out of strength rather then weakness or dependence.

So this process is going to be difficult but unless you are prepared to take the risk nothing is going to change. Remember you have to decide. Live each day as a new day- living by faith means to look to Him each day to guide you and lead you. This is adventure, this is empowerment - not being dragged down by failures and guilt of the past - but living in the cleansing power of the blood and now by faith being powered to move forward knowing that as you do so God is with you to direct your steps. New thoughts will emerge - you are always thinking ahead - not being stuck in old ways of thinking and doing but being creative to manage change and come up with new solutions to old dilemmas and therefore being creative and productive. This is the essence of life - creativity.

Coping

When Jesus is in control He puts His compassion into the relationship. His wisdom to solve problems. There is no need to battle over control for He is in charge of your life.

BEHAVIOURS

SOCIAL NETWORK		**GENETICS**
EXPERIENCES	**FEELINGS**	**LIFE**
EVENTS		
CULTURE	**THOUGHTS**	**FAMILY**
	HABITS	

How all this in interaction effects the production of an individual. Culture shapes ones life. Genetics- the things that make one vulnerable to disorder and disease. Life events that precipitate or are insults to make a person have a breakdown. There are so many factors but an individual's habitual way of coping is what needs to be addressed. These ways of coping - fight or flight than determines if one will be able to cope or not. Growth is a constant experience of change. When a person is able to adapt to changing circumstances and pressures then one has learnt how to do so from within. The pressures from outside will come and go but when a person lives from a solid identity from within then one is able to overcome all hindrances. This needs constant working in the internal machinery. Time to reflect and to sharpen the saw. Too much activity drains one. It's good to separate from the routine of daily life and begin to go inward to allow the Spirit to cleanse and to fill and to revitalise. All areas of your being need to work in harmony. This harmony comes from a unity between mind and spirit. The body just follows. It's in this area that resources are replenished to be able to function as a person. When there is no unity then one resorts to denial and projection that leads to one being blind to oneself to those areas of oneself that is projected on to others. So let the Holy Spirit do His work in you to unite the left and the right through the Cross. This is the dilemma of each person. The bad seems to dictate - the power of sin and guilt. The Cross of Jesus has cancelled this power. His blood cleanses you of the guilt - a consequence of the power of sin. Now you are free to be. Now the God part of you can prevail over the flesh part of you. As long as you live this flesh part of you will tempt and entice you to choose the quick and easy way. The Godly way is through patience and perseverance.

Experience

The things that last are learnt through experiences. So don't major on injunctions but try and translate them into experience - story telling mode. This captures the mind and the emotions, which is what experience is all about. A mere intellectual discourse does not affect the heart and so disappears. What invokes the emotions will have a lasting effect on the senses. This is why boy/girl relationships are like temporary madness. All logic goes out of the window because the feelings take over. One is driven by the stimulant effects of romantic love (lust). One's perception changes and everything has a glow in it, it's so positive. The negatives seem to be forgotten. This kind of love is temporary. God's love has these components but is based on a different premise. God's love is unconditional. It is not based on feelings but promises. Gods love judges and redeems. God's love is everlasting.
So learn to build your life on the Words of life. Jesus words contain life. This is the born again experience. His words entered and were received with joy and this touched your feelings and life came forth. It's His life now that attracts you. Life's contradictions were suddenly solved through the Cross. Justice and mercy were reconciled and out came Christ in resurrection power to save, heal and deliver one from the clutches of sin. This is the gospel - the good news.
Now as I receive this Truth - Jesus into the deep parts of my being - I am changed to be His disciple. He does it as I walk by

faith looking to His Spirit who gives me the understanding, faith and power to do what is impossible for me to do.

So death and life is at work in me. Death to my old life as I choose His life. His life in me is constantly keeping me from the fleeting pleasures of sin. I am committed to Him and therefore I am discipled by Him. He comes to me and restores me and replenishes me. He gives me wisdom and knowledge I need to live a life of hope and vitality and strength.

False guilt

False guilt is a curse that the devil uses to bind people to believing something that is not real. False guilt is the product of imaginations. Imaginations are fed by the evil one. He causes you to imagine evil, lustful thoughts. This is the way he attacks you. Then you succumb to the lustful or evil thoughts and he makes you feel that you have committed the offence. In other cases you feel guilty because someone else suffers and you take the blame. These are due to the ways one thinks. False guilt needs to be separated from real guilt. Real guilt should lead to repentance. False guilt is not real and therefore tends to plague one. It's like all imagination. We are fallen beings and therefore prone to sinful thoughts. However we can choose whether we will entertain them or not. It's the choice that makes the difference in every area of our life.

False guilt like everything that is not of the truth has the purpose to cripple people. This needs to be faced. Childhood traumas and reactions that are not based on real facts but illusions of the real. Parental loyalties and other controlling and manipulating acts tend to instil this false guilt. If we allow false guilt to control us then we become crippled.

Controlling and domineering parents tend to cause their children to feel guilty to keep them under control. This then becomes a part of adult life. Therefore when we try to stand up to authority figures this guilt arises and paralyses us into inaction. This is how dictators have been able to control masses of people by making them feel guilty.

The power of false guilt is as real guilt. This is because it has to go through the same process of thinking. The mind does not differentiate between the false and the true. Feelings are evoked whatever the source. The mind only responds to the thought whether fact or fiction- false or true. So be careful to differentiate between the real and the imaginary. A lot of people have imaginary fears. These fears were instilled in them as a child. It's the adult that needs to now face the fear based on facts. The child then is enabled to face the fear with the help of the adult. People operate as adults in the thinking area but at feeling level they behave like children. For the feelings to change the adult must make the decisions. Then he must act on those decisions and the feelings will change. This is the path to emotional growth. So the adult will operate from the adult position and not allow the emotional fears, guilt and sadness of the child to dominate the adult life.

Facing your fears

This kind of change needs insight to the operations of the mind. By faith in God one can move out into unknown territories and face the fears. The fears are not out there. They are inside the individual. So once the fears are faced in real life then the new information will challenge childhood fears and healing will occur. Firstly these fears will have to be acknowledged. Secondly they need to be confronted.
We are all creatures of habit. Therefore our habitual responses will always dominate and control our responses. It takes time and effort to change our responses. This is done by choice. The adult thinks and chooses not to respond in habitual ways but by doing what an adult should do. This will break familial patterns. This needs the individual to step back from behaviours that were acceptable in families and made one feel part of a family or group and begin to make choices to operate as an individual from ones true centre. This takes courage. But by faith one is able to do anything.
Jesus Christ took this position. He spoke the Truth and this upset the powers to be. He turned the world right side up. The world was so introverted, thinking of no.1 and controlling others to conform. He came to liberate the individual to be a person - free and responsible for one's actions. When one loses

this choice then one becomes a victim of the system.
True freedom and liberty is within an individual. This is what leads to growth and a sense of vision and mission.

Superficial need vs. deeper needs

To discern rightly is to understand the spirit behind the words. God judges the heart of man. A lot of conflict is not related to heart issues but on superficial differences. When one is drawn into the conflict through what is seen or heard ie. the senses, then one has missed the point. The superficial is to lead one to the deeper issues. The deeper issues have to be addressed at the heart level. However work on the superficial needs to happen for the superficial is a barrier to getting to the heart of the matter. Therefore a child who soils not only has a problem with his soiling but also has to deal with his parent's anger and frustration. The parents have to deal with the soiling and their own frustration and anger. The soiling can be seen as a symptom of a deeper issue like rejection or unlove. The symptom or problem is linked or fired by this emotion. The emotion may never be addressed yet it can be dealt with by addressing the problem and dealing with the anger it arouses in the parents and child. So the problem serves as a vehicle- talking point to address the deeper issue of rejection. Many times this is the only way of addressing the deeper issues. The deeper issues are difficult to grasp or handle but the symptom can be grasped. So symptoms or behaviours do give one a lot of information. What factors resulted in the symptom may not be the same that maintains the symptom. So change needs to be directed to both the forces that maintain the symptom and those that gave rise to it. This kind of linkage enables one to intervene at several points to bring about change.

A lot of management work addresses problems at the systemic level or maintaining factors. Deeper work at an individual level will enable or empower the individual to take control of their life. Empowering individuals will enable them to address the deeper issues within themselves to prevent problems arising. The splits, alliances and coalitions that occur are a result of ways people respond to threat and fear. The group is cemented through the common fear or threat. This coming together enables the individuals to feel safe in the midst of the real or perceived threat. This fear then controls the group and therefore the individuals within the group. Its only when the fear and the response to the fear is addressed that the group is released from the crippling emotion.

Emotions have to be addressed or faced up to for what they are. Defences tend to mask the emotion and through denial and projection place the blame on others. These kinds of mechanisms lead to a mentality of exclusion ie. splitting of those bits that can be blamed. In an organisation this is usually the management. The management is responsible for the induction of the fear and they are to be blamed. The management's response can be in anger or understanding. An understanding response leads to alliance. A polarised response fuels the fear even more.

So in all areas of relationships this kind of phenomenon arises. It's one's response to these situations that leads to coping or collapse. To cope is to be able to manage these situations in a way that leads to solutions. Difference gives rise to tension. The tension must then lead one to look at ways to come up with creative solutions that is better than fixed roles and structures. So in the work situation the crisis will result in dismantling previously strongly held, stuck in the mud positions, to one of managing as a group- as a team to come up with solutions. The discipline identity is sacrificed for the sake of the whole. This shift will give rise to a different dynamic. The dynamic shift is to address the deeper personal issue that interferes with the functioning as a member of the team. In a crisis one either withdraws into more role definition or allows the crisis to lead one to operate or grow into a higher level of functioning to cope with the crisis. There are two forces at work- one to regress to the state of security with the familiar or to push oneself upward to a higher level of functioning that leads to a more responsive and accountable person. This kind of person or team will be high on responsibility and able to speak for oneself and not be gripped by fear to conform to the social mirror. Leaders have to be of

this calibre to lead people to this higher level of functioning. The structures then that are formed reinforce this kind of healthier functioning.
So also in families, crises should lead to persons being more responsible and accountable and not regress to be stuck in their roles. In church too these crises lead to people becoming much more accountable and not be taken up by the voice of the most charismatic or popular person or group. In all this there is a middle ground. It's the pull to occupy extreme positions that leads to conflict and polarisation. It's the willingness to understand that leads to compromise and therefore operating closer to reality. Jesus and His Word can never be compromised. His Word is eternal. His truth can never change. However it's our response that needs to change. One can take an intellectual stance to the truth or a heart response. It's the balance of the two; so that the heart response also takes into account the maturational stage or level of development of the individual or group. This is where compromise occurs. It is not a compromise of standards but the rationalisation of the ideal and the real. What is ideal may not be achievable. Therefore the realistic goals have to be set to achieve that which is achievable.

Emotionally free

To be emotionally free is to not be plagued by feelings and thoughts that are sensitive to deep needs of having to be loved and respected. To be free emotionally is to be able to relate with others as persons separate from oneself. Others will feel free from any force of being manipulated to meet your need for love or significance. You will feel free to be yourself and there won't be any pretence. You will relate with others as a human being and others will be free to relate with you as one. You will not be affected by the reactions of others for you will see the need in others and not their reactions, which are a cover up for their need or deprivation.
This is only possible as you become attached to Christ. Your emotional needs can only be met in Christ. This is why you need to surrender wholly to Him. This is a continuous walk

with Him 24 hours - taking up your cross saying no to your own needs and looking to Him to meet your needs. This is the only way Christ can meet your needs. For any other way will lead to self-glorification. The flesh has to die daily. It is dead but you must apply this truth daily. Everything is made available to you through the Cross-ie. His death has freed you from the power of sin. Now His resurrection power is available to you to rise up in the fruits and gifts of the Spirit. It is the Holy Spirit that manifests these in you as you acknowledge Jesus as Lord. The Father gives freely in Jesus Name. The Holy Spirit then provides the power to receive. Without the Holy Spirit you cannot receive anything. That's why an intimate relationship with the Holy Spirit will enable you to be led into the land of Canaan- of milk and honey for spirit soul and body. It starts in the spirit and it affects the soul and the body.
It's because man has forgotten or is blind to the spirit that he gropes in darkness. The god of this world has blinded the eyes of man to the realm of the spirit. So he is lost and gropes in the light he has. Now is the time to rise up in faith in Jesus and His finished work on the Cross and to defeat your enemies. This power is released to you as you step out in faith and speak the word into existence. The Holy Spirit will touch your tongue and what you say will come to pass- blessing or curse. So be careful to walk in the blood of Jesus and to speak forth the Word of His power in boldness.

Becoming what you imagine

God's love is what transforms the individual. Pentecost is the personal experience of Gods love invading an individual to transform an individual from within. This is only possible when one desires and yearns for this experience of total surrender to God and control by Him. This means saying no to ones own desires and looking to God. If I am energised by this vision to be like Jesus then I will give up all things to be like Him to make real the vision. Paul's vision was to be like Him. Each man becomes like what he imagines. The heart always dictates what we become. Therefore it is heart attitudes that need to change. There is no other way.

Giving up is to be prepared to change. Holding on is to keep to what is familiar. This is not healthy. Change and difference brings about the need to grow to meet the challenge. Where there is no challenge there will be no change. In a changing environment there needs to be some flexibility to meet the challenge of changes. Therefore one remains flexible to bend and to move in a way a dancer moves. One is not like a robot fixed in its range of movements. One moves from the heart. The heart is not separated from the head. It's when the head dictates with no consultation with the heart that a schism arises. This schism then creates a feeling of unreality, which leads to breakdown.

Head and heart unity

The heart and head need to flow together; in this is unity, synthesis and creativity. The head decides and the body follows in action. However if the heart is not involved then the action feels robot like.

Pentecost is a fresh instillation of God's love and power into the soul that cleanses the soul and empowers it to connect with the spirit and head. The soul needs to be changed. The soul is the receptacle of all thoughts, memories and feelings of years of patterning, maps and pain that needs to be cleansed, freed and let loose to receive the anointing. The anointing comes in as I let go and let God come in and do His work. The Holy Spirit is the transformer, the Spirit of Jesus. When the Spirit of Jesus comes then you become like Him. The Spirit of Jesus comes only when all other spirits are released from the place in your life. You hold the key. Now release yourself from their control. Let your will be released to the Father just as Jesus said your will be done. Now let the Holy Spirit come and take control of the wheel (will) to guide you, teach you, comfort you and help you, to do what is pleasing in His sight.

With the heart a man intuits and is able to know God. It's when a man walks in unison with his heart that he walks in unity, synchrony and feels alive. When the heart and mind are split from each other then he feels like a robot - playing the role. It appears ok. but it is just a role. People are caught up in acting roles - acting the part - anyone with some insight can see it for what it is. Roles are important to carry out functions but can't replace the person. It is the person behind the role that is important. Very few come in touch with this person. Many play the role but are not aware of them. It's only in crisis that the real state of the true self is known. God desires that I become present to my true self. When a person does not address the needs of the real self, then a false self is created with it's desires and wishes that are based on false premises. This false self is shaped by circumstances ie. if the real self is rejected then the false self sets up images to make up for this rejection by investing in one's work, talents or hobbies or in addiction to lessen the pain.

True integration

To be present at all times - united, integrated being - able to differentiate the inner world from the outer - having a security and a resonance that is deep and congruent with internal reality. Not being an actor but having a synchronous relationship that resonates like a well tuned musical instrument sounding it's notes clearly so that others can hear and not be confused - this is true integration - of all my faculties - the physical, emotional and spiritual being in tune - not just following a doctrine or value blindly but truly integrating it into my spirit, soul and body. Jesus Christ is Lord of all - letting this knowledge seep into my being till my whole being resonates - principle of love, peace, kindness, joy - these need to be programmed into my brain - emotional responses - empowerment - action.

Expectations

Expect from God. Don't be limited by your own expectations. If you want to go beyond yourself and the goals of this limited worldview then you must centre yourself in God. God is above all. So when you centre in Him His resources are released to infuse your mind and your spirit with knowledge and wisdom and power to achieve His goals. This is only possible as you die to your own selfish and fallen desires and submit yourself to Him. Don't be afraid. He will lead you in the way of peace. You must be ready to do anything He commands. This is true freedom. To choose to allow God to dictate in your life. If you want to release yourself, to free yourself from your own set ways of thinking and doing then you must allow God to lead you and direct you in all areas of your life. Wait on Him. This is the only way. When you come to the place where you cannot do anything without His approval, this is the place of true freedom. You have made a choice for God. Choosing to do it your way only leads to reinventing the old patterns. These patterns are ego syntonic and therefore are not a threat to you. However God's ways are not always your way. This is how change occurs. You may have to go it alone in the physical but your faith and trust is in God. You will say Lord I submit, Holy Spirit come and direct me and power is released to you. Submission is true humility - this combined with a call, a cry to God will bring His resources. Many have lost their way and travelled in the wilderness because of a failure to receive this simple truth. They have chosen to go their own way.

Just as fasting is a form of death- a dying to the flesh- so also in all areas. A dying to have ones own way releases God's resources to fill the gap so created. ie, I give up that God may come in to possess. Waiting for God to do what He desires is like this. Failure has the same effect. You have failed - now God can have His way. True success is not in having ones own way but Gods way. Jesus did not face the Cross as an end in itself. He knew that He had to die so that He could save others. This same principle applies in all areas. Only death can bring forth the resurrection power of God.

This is the constant struggle you will have to face. All through life there are choices that have to be made. Wait therefore till you know what is right to do. Wait is the operative word.

Fantasy and idealised relationships

Fantasy can be a form of reality for some but this is not the real thing. Fantasy is based on wishes. These wishes are usually not possible but it gives a certain narcissistic gratification. This arises from the fallen position. These fantasies arise from the hurt child who resorts to fantasy to make up for the loss or hurt. Emotions get connected to the fantasy so much so that the inner child prefers to spend time enjoying the fantasy then the reality. Fantasy does not entertain negatives. It blows the image, the object of fantasy out of proportion and imbues it with qualities it does not have. This kind of idealisation makes the object of the fantasy even more attractive. It makes up for the deprived rejected inner child. Because the need for love has not been met in reality therefore the inner child replaces this with a fantasy object - usually another person who is not present but is imbued with qualities that preserve the fantasy. This kind of thinking replaces the deepest need of man to have a relationship that is deep and meaningful. This can only be provided by God. However God is so distant that there is no relationship with Him in reality. Therefore fantasy images take His place.

Deep emotional needs can be met through relationships only. However relationships are painful. They are in the now and both positive and negative qualities need to be accepted in any relationship. If primary attachments have been disturbed then future relationships are going to suffer. Therefore the child withdraws into fantasy. This fantasy is an escape from the present and also keeps hope alive for the future. If nothing else the fantasy object fulfils the deep need for love although it is only in fantasy. It's the positive emotions associated with the fantasy that keeps it alive and the inner child is fed through the positive emotions that are aroused in the inner child. This is unreality but some live all their lives in this fantasy world because reality is too painful. They may superficially present as okay but their inner world is poor and deprived but for fantasy images.

Character building

The real quality of an inner life is seen in character. Nothing can replace this. True character is born out of the struggle with the inner pressures of good and evil. When a person

makes choices based on the true principles of good then he builds character in himself. Good character building results in love, patience and self-control. A lack of basic security in the inner self results in a chasing after every new doctrine and fad but fails to address the deep inner need for love and significance.
Only God can fill the emptiness of a soul that is deprived. This deprivation is so deep and cannot be met by another human being other then through Gods love through a God filled person.

Motivation

Motivation is the key to any successful venture. If the motivation is for someone other then oneself then there is hope. All self-centred motivation will run into trouble. This is especially so if one is entering a venture to boost ones own morale or self esteem or credit points. This is because if ones own self esteem is down it is very prone to pull everything down with it. Therefore if the motivation is in oneself the project will go up and down dependent on the mood state of the individual concerned. THAT'S WHY THE OBJECT OF MOTIVATION MUST BE FROM OUTSIDE. THIS WILL BE THE INSPIRING SOURCE. FOR SOME IT IS THE GOAL. However all these are short lived till the goal is reached. For motivation to be a life principle it needs to be of eternal quality. Faith in God is one motivating principle. A desire to follow Jesus is a motivating principle. Therefore no matter what happens it is not dependent on earthly goals or objectives or even in self but in One who is other then self or any earthly object.

The Holy Spirit inspires and fires up your faith each time you call on Him. You become so fired up with His vision, His zeal, and His desires that they overtake and overcome you. Then you are not dictated by earthly pressures, whims and fancies but by an eternal source that never fails.

Motivation is a life principle. A boy falling in love is motivated by love, passion or lust for the object of his love. Emotions come into it. Emotions are the driving force. The will is set on the object of the motivation. The emotion and the intellect come into line with the will. Action occurs and plans and targets are set to achieve the goal. However the goals themselves are not the end in themselves. There is a greater and higher goal- to be like the Master, to fulfil His mission in life, to be the vessel God created me for. A man possessed by God is able to do mighty things he never dreamed was possible.

Acceptance

Openness is a characteristic of a man who has accepted himself for who he is. He is not caged by social expectations but by the fact that he is a sinner saved by grace. This is the change that needs to occur. Sin is a universal fact that affects every man and woman and child. These limits vary from one culture to another. They are not universal. A man who has come to accept his own sinfulness and realises and has experienced Gods forgiveness is truly free. Sin is a reality but so is freedom. What he chooses to operate in makes the difference between how he operates - in sin and bondage or in deliverance and freedom.

Acceptance of self and others

So stop getting into defensive behaviour or the wish to be somebody else - God has called you to be you - accept yourself as you are. Others may feel different but you need to live according to what you know is best. I am therefore I can, I will, I believe. This is the essence of true liberty. Then you draw the boundary between self and others. You don't get into situations of demanding, manipulative and possessive behaviours. It is only an independent person who will be able to relate well with others. Otherwise there is a danger of entering into relationships that either robs oneself of wholeness or the other. Mutual needs attract people to each other. However, this attraction then leads to a merging of identities. This merging then leads to threats of loss or abandonment, which then leads to clingy behaviour. No one else is allowed to enter the relationship because of fear.

People who spend too much time in fantasy find that many times that what they fantasise does not meet up with reality. This then is the cause of frustration, which leads to further escape into fantasy. The solution is to accept one self and ones circumstances and position in life and to live to the full in it. This is the only way or path to self-improvement. From here one can move forward to achieve in the real world than in fantasy. In the real world what is done is what will bring forth fruit. Fantasising, dreaming has its place but should be seen as a means to productive action otherwise it remains in the realm of the unreal. What is real is seen, heard and felt. Action in this realm is what will lead to real change. Therefore it is action that is required. Mere fantasy will not have the same effect as doing or acting.

One can plan a line of action but must do it to attain change. Confusion can many times, be the springboard to action. So do not be worried or alarmed, only let the confusion lead you to seek for solutions. Problems are opportunities for creative solutions - for growth, for achievement, for success.

Labelling

Words are only words if they are not applicable to life situations. The solution must be congruent to the situation and to the people. The problem is not the person. The problem is affecting the person. Therefore it is only when the problem can be separated from the person that the person is able to do anything about it. Stealing is a problem but when the problem becomes the person - a thief than the person is unable to do anything about it. This is the issue in labelling. Therefore the first task is to identify the problem. The next task is to distance the problem from the person. The next is to empower the person who is now distanced from the problem and is able to attack the problem ie. separate his identity from the problem. The problem is then cut off from its life source (the person) and will die. Empowering of individuals to confront the problem is a powerful way of defeating the problem and setting the victim free.

We are all victims of our past and present circumstances. Only as we distance ourselves from our past will we be able to do something about our present. Just like sin, the past keeps us fixed in our positions. Spiritual experiences, positive life events, brings in a difference that then creates a situation that enables the victim to separate himself from the past and the circumstances and perceptions of others that then leads to deliverance.

Gods solution is His Son- His blood to cleanse- this is a spiritual operation that has effects on the soul and the body. Society colludes with evil by giving into sinful ways for the sake of the person. A Christian does not condemn the person but the sin that results in the sinful behaviour. It's the effects of sin that are seen in the biological, emotional and social situations. God's answer applies to all situations. His blood can reverse the biological disturbances, which will affect the soul and the environment - society as a whole.

Sin

Many are bound through sickness of the soul. The sickness of the soul is sin. Sin keeps you bound through fear. Faith releases you from fear - fear of others and fear of the future. The only way out of this is to receive the love of God through faith. His love will drive out all past and present fear. Then hope, the vital, curative, exponential force will enable you to face the future, optimistic that He who has called you to a job will see you through to the end. He is in you. Now live life to the full. Facts are just the list of things about the truth. Truth is in the spirit. Without the spirit, man is dead. Therefore neglecting the spirit is like words without power. The dunamis power is in the spirit. If you don't have the Spirit of God in you then your words are as good as a parrot that repeats the words but because they are out of context is devoid of meaning. It's the context that provides the meaning that then enables one to change by changing the template that is causing the problem. Meaning is unique to the individual. So the opinions of people are important. It is when a man speaks from his heart that meaning flows. Otherwise it's just empty words. A deprived heart cannot release life. Life is not in the words but in the person who speaks the words. Therefore beware of words and who speaks them -they have the power to curse or bless.

Opening up to God's resources

God is able if I trust him to help me in all my endeavours. All I need to do is to completely trust Him. I will think and do as if I am totally free, for in this way I make myself totally vulnerable and open to learn and to win. If I let my fear cage me, then I become a recluse not open to God's love and to people. I open up my brain - like a 747 opens up its' hold to let its' cargo in. So I open up my mind to receive God's thoughts - creative thoughts - new ideas, solutions and thoughts of wisdom to solve intractable problems. All this in an attitude of love, resourcefulness, positive, possibility thinking - not limited to frames of reference that are absolute, linked to opinions and group culture but to innovative possibilities, creative, new and refreshing. Some frameworks are for learning and others are to help give one direction. Once you are free you enter into God's frame of reference - this is beyond human boundaries - open to other possibilities that bring in God's resources - ideas that unleash new power to overcome and cross over mountains and terrains that at one time seemed impossible. It's to fly like an eagle - to see from above - to scale the heights with no fear because my confidence is in God Almighty. I will love and give so that I extend myself beyond myself to touch others. As long as I am closed I will not learn and grow. Plants that are kept in a bottle are kept small. In an open environment one has all the space to expand. So closed environments are not conducive to growth. The open spaces are the places to be for there is fresh air, freedom and ability to move freely. So structure is important only to enable the family to keep to set limits so that the children are safe and can grow but once they are grown up they need to be forced to decide on their own life goals. The old structure must change to accommodate this. Yet it is the emotional traits that lead to restriction. Fears, negative thoughts keep a person caged in a structure that inhibits growth and learning. Once the basics have been learnt then there must be room for creativity otherwise life becomes a routine chore, which kills.

Self esteem

Having a good self-esteem is important. This does not mean that having a good self-esteem appears to be a rejection of dependence on God. Self-esteem is to be able to live comfortably with one self - to accept one self as I am. This then enables me to grow. If I cannot accept myself then I will always be putting myself down and giving over my life to fears, worries and others. Jesus came to set me free from this internal conflict. His Cross serves the purpose of cancelling out this internal conflict so that there is peace. Without this peace, the negative will try to assume control. Only the Cross has the power to cancel the power of negative control.

The neurotics prison

A neurotic has a low sense of self. He is a slave to the worrying dreams within himself - demons of fear, shame, guilt, poverty, rebellion and control. These demons seek to destroy the individual. The Cross and the blood come to deliver, cleanse and free the individual from these negative forces. The positive power of God in Christ Jesus is able to extinguish these forces of the mind and heart and set the prisoner free. This freedom is internal. Many hide their conflicts of pain with externals. Externals cannot free a person. This freedom cannot be bought with money. Only Christ can set a person free. A person needs to be born again to be free. The new birth is the way out of neurotic conflict.

It all starts at the time of birth - the relationships with parents that set the stage for future relationships. Relationships are just a reflection of one's state (internal). So one can judge one's state through ones' relationships. When one is free, one is able to relate with all - no prejudices - able to tolerate other's differences and not fear difference. A person who cannot cope with difference is one who is insecure and therefore retreats into his shell where he is safe in a sense, in a fence or a prison of false security. The negative forces within serve to keep the victims imprisoned for life. It is only a person who is able to reach out to these victims who can restore the sense of self in the other. This requires time, patience and perseverance till the blighted soul develops trust and faith to take the risk of venturing out into a hard and hostile world.

Addictions

Addictions arise because there is a compulsion fired by demons to kill or destroy the real self. Everything false is of the evil one. The person has opened themselves up to false desires based on rejection, hurt and resentment and therefore has opened themselves up to demonic activity. This activity is then embraced because of its seductive quality. All major crimes started with some rejection or slight that took on other qualities that drive the person to commit the crime. All these need the healing balm of Jesus. Who can meet that need, that deep heart felt need - only Jesus. Many therapies claim to bring us to a consciousness or release from the overpowering feelings but none can relieve and release the captive from his torment. It can be given a different name but what is in a name. Only when the deeper needs are met is the person released or free to be a person.

Friendship

The ability to think and feel for others is the secret of friendship. Narcissism is the worst form of personality disorder. Only death to self is able to free one from these selfish tendencies to wholeness in Christ. This death is a death to the flesh - the old man with his old ways of thinking and feeling that needs to be crucified daily so that the new life in Christ can be operational. This is a process. By faith one takes this position in Christ. Then the Holy Spirit gets to work to cleanse, heal and deliver. The other way is through psychotherapy - the fleshly way of working through. Many can't go through with this process because it is threatening and also painful. The main problem is fear. One gets used to routine forms of thinking and doing even if it is unhelpful. To then let down one's guard and try new ways is threatening. This is what psychotherapy is all about. To change the defences that keep a person imprisoned to a form of thinking and doing that keeps the person chained to himself. It is as if a person is caged in and the cage is the defence. When a person is free then he can walk out of his cage but will need other ways of coping that are new. This takes a walk of faith. But this is only possible if one has faith in God the Father to take control or take care. If there isn't this trust then one will go back to his or her familiar ways of doing things. The familiar is more comfortable than the new and unknown.

Influences

Families, groups, tend to mould a person to act and behave in certain ways. So when one is in a group one tends to copy or fit in with the behaviour of that group. When one is in a different setting then other ways of coping come into line. These are the ways in which one relates and behaves. The less opportunity for interaction with others the less opportunity for change. Therefore it is important that one keeps company with others otherwise it's so easy to withdraw into ones shell and be safe.

Security

A secure person does not need to react because his security does not come from what other people think but from within. If it is going to be it is up to me - always. If I place my success on what other people say or think then I am no more in control. In God I am always victorious because I am a winner in Him - for He has said so. Opinions come and go - they are not facts - so don't let opinions be your judge - rather in all matters you be your own judge and critic - in this way you will choose to grow and not allow others to choose for you. This is the narrow path and so few choose to walk in it.

Attitudes

Attitudes are so important. A wrong attitude can so sour a situation, pollute the atmosphere, cause people to withdraw, lead to negativism, backbiting and hostility. It is important to have a spark that will light the positive fires and extinguish the climate of negativity so that it can be burnt off. The positive spark of positive attitudes and possibility thinking can spark off positive feelings in a place of death and gloom.
It is attitudes that lead to a changed lifestyle. All other change is in terms of buildings and external changes. Internal changes only occur as attitudes change. External change is cosmetic. The people within the home are the same. True change occurs only when ones attitude changes. This cannot be bought with money - it has to do with habits. Old habits continue to have a powerful influence. These only change with concerted effort to change. Man is a creature of routine. His habits tend to determine his actions. Only a change to better himself, can he change to see the future differently. Otherwise the same is replicated. Jesus came to change the heart of man so that he can now begin to change directions to a heavenly goal. Hallelujah. Jesus is alive. I will trust in Him. I will look to Him to guide me and lead me. It is this change that will change perceptions.

Positive attitude

A positive attitude always attracts. I will be a positive source of blessing to all. Positive attracts positive. I will stimulate the endorphins by praise - through praise. Praise is the aggressive energy of the spirit and the soul. I can only praise when I am totally submitted to him. I then acknowledge His rule over my life. I remain submitted and committed to His rule over my life. I therefore am not concerned about what happens around me. I shall look to Him and praise Him. All negatives I just confess. When I am not positive then I come and kneel down at the foot of the Cross and repent and confess and cut myself free from the demon of anger, envy, lust, control and all negativity that will seek to assault me. Whatever the source I will be positive.

Positive praise extinguishes the negative flames - like water to fire. Praise keeps my eyes on Jesus. I cleanse myself. Praise will not attract any negatives. It is only a negative state of mind that will attract negativity from others and from the atmosphere. So it is so essential to keep on praising. Offer up a sacrifice of praise.

Change of attitude

Change of attitude leads to change of behaviour - greatest discovery in this century. Man is able to do this if only he is ready to be open. A closed up mind is trapped in it's programming. I need to listen to others and not be afraid. In listening to others I am open to change. The ability to listen is an indication of the ability to learn and grow. If one does not listen or will not then what I indicate is that I am closed up. I have found my false sense of security in my own world and am not prepared to expose myself to others lest I am challenged, made vulnerable, made insecure or proved wrong or a failure etc. So to be free I need to be open to challenge. This is the only way to grow. Even failure is another opening. I have been exposed to the light and the darkness (deception) will be exposed and I will be set free. People are not prepared for change. I must live in the knowledge of Gods' love. It is His light that enables me to walk in the light and not fear. The fear of man is an indication of a lack of security in the love of God. Where the love of God has not penetrated the darkness of the soul then man will build a kingdom within based on his fears. The fears will build walls that will imprison self. The walls are - power, pleasures, material goods, status, pride etc that will collapse in the day of trouble for fear within will be exposed and the walls of power, material goods and fame will not be able to sustain you. So trust in the Lord. He is the only One who can sustain you. In Him you are truly free. Monetary freedom is not true freedom. You may have all the freedom you need but what if you are confronted with death - the chief enemy of the soul. So don't be deceived - only God can give you the security to keep you focused on what is important.

Mind sets

Mind sets - this is what it is all about. You mind set will determine how you see yourself, others and the world. A negative mind set will see impurity or evil in every behaviour or act. A positive mindset will see the good, even the negatives will be seen as good and can believe that all things work for good. Proactive thinking has capitalised on this. This has improved peoples self image - possibility thinking - power thinking. Christ has called us to be a positive people. This is the attraction - that it builds people up - it feeds the psychological self. The positive gospel of Jesus Christ has not changed the negative mindset of people. Why? Because the teaching of the church has not built people up but condemned them. When the positive gospel of Jesus Christ is combined with a positive self-image it leads to explosion. This is the missing link in the church. People are starved in this area. There is confusion between the old self and the renewed self. The renewed self is condemned with the old self. There is therefore no self - this then leads to a negative mindset where one is always putting one self down in the name of humility. But true humility is not to put one self down but to serve others and to be served. I need help, is a true state of a humble heart. This struggle is what splits people into groups. For a person to be successful there needs to be an integrity of thoughts, feelings, values and goals. A conflict in these areas leads to disappointment. People fight others because it does not synchronise with their own beliefs or challenge them. Ignorance, misinformation leads to these situations. How the positive power of God can so spark people to new heights. When one considers this it becomes so apparent that all the conflicts are due to threats and fears. A positive self-image can cope with differences. It is my position to be positive - this is the only way I can win others. I need to be sure of my position whatever others may say. Then I associate with people who are like-minded. This is why humans form into groups.

All negativity will flow out as I embrace the positive. I am attracted to negative only because of the negative self-image. A negative self-image attracts negatives - and this rules on one.

It needs a positive self-image to cancel the negative.

Think

Think, think, and think. Very important to think otherwise will operate on rote, which is like a robot, and life becomes boring and stale.
You are loved and you know your eternal destiny is secure - so go and enjoy life. Live freely - no fear, for your Master looks after you - this is belief - it is this belief that will see you through whenever doubts or fears or anxiety pass by, know that what you think and believe is what will come to pass. Thinking and believing for success will bring success. Don't be sidetracked by the minutiae at this point. It is the global view that is important. Getting stuck in non-essentials or in the minutiae leads to a investment of energy in the wrong place. So whenever you feel yourself getting stuck in the minutiae - anxiety increases and you become narrow in your focus - then step back and look at the larger picture - to the context and this will bring other information to your assistance which then can solve or resolve the problem. So always keep the larger picture in mind when you get stuck in the minutiae because then your emotions get triggered off- mainly fear and anxiety - which then paralyses your thought processes. Living by faith is to walk into the unknown knowing that God is with you and will give you the knowledge and wisdom you require when you require it.

Positive thinking

Positive thinking enables one to free oneself from the negative ruts of childhood programming and emotional responses and behaviours. This is the way forward. Christ came to give us abundant life - the abundant life is experienced as one chooses to forsake and abandon the old and choose the new.
It's the security of knowledge in Christ that enables me to be. Evil will just melt away in the positive knowledge and power of God. Others become attracted to a change in message. Everyone is attracted to this message of hope. All can come

with their negativity knowing that Christ has died for all. This is the message the world needs to hear.

How solutions come forth as I move out in faith. The more I do so the more faith I have in all situations - always knowing and believing that if one door is shut a better one is waiting to open up - so I need goals but I must wait for God's timing and His way is always the best way - this is adventure, creativity, challenge, life.

When I know that God is in control - I just rest in this knowledge and learn to be myself - always improving myself - pushing myself to be excellent.

Perceptions

Once the children have been taught the principles of life, then they need to be released to find out for themselves what is good. They will choose the influences in life that will enable them to resist the forces of evil and choose the good. The best the parents can do at this point is to teach them to make the right choices - choices that will build them up and not tear them down. Choices that will be win /win solutions rather than win/lose solutions. To be able to always think of the other - for it is more important that the other person's respect for himself is preserved then making one over him/her. Many in this world suffer because they have a low opinion of themselves. It is only Gods' love, solid and sure that can ensure that they don't give up on themselves. It is so important to view every human being as Gods' creation - not from the outward form but in the likeness of God. This is so essential. For no other perception can evoke a compassion for others like the compassion of Christ for the sinner. So be still and do not be distracted by the forces within and without that will tempt you to give up. Rather let the Spirit of God so soften your heart. The hardness of heart comes from being careless in allowing the forces in this world to so influence your mind that it becomes difficult to absorb the love of God to soften it. It is only the Spirit of God who can so penetrate through this hardness. There is a softness in the centre but this vulnerable self cannot be healed because of the hardness of the shell. It is only when the shell is broken that the tender inner self can be touched. The hard shell preserves the vulnerable self from the evil and negativity of this world. It is this self that needs to be touched and healed. Everyone has this soft centre covered by the hardness of roles, riches, position, honours, race etc. At the centre, every human being is the same and needs the love of Christ that can heal and restore. So keep this in mind always. Do not allow the insults and assaults of others harden you but allow these to help you see the sensitive nature of others. It is only hardened people that are critical, sceptical and cold. So beware of your own inclination to judge - judge yourself, love heals all - so let love be the source, purpose and goal of your life - to love is to be like Jesus.

Paradigms shifts

Paradigm shifts - poverty to abundance. God works on paradigms. When I fit into Gods paradigm - it effects my whole being. This is a true conversion experience - it is a shift from a sinner to a saint. From a poverty stricken, fearful mentality - to a generous, abundance mentality. I can love - because Gods riches are limitless. It's the true richness within oneself that leads to riches without. I am rich because Jesus Christ the Saviour of the world dwells in me. It is His riches that will lead me to think abundantly and live abundantly.
Poverty of spirit > poverty of mind > poverty in strength. Abundance in spirit > abundance mentality > strength in body. This shift needs to occur. However if the abundance in spirit has not followed with abundance in thinking - somehow the fullness in spirit is not associated with a abundance mentality. It is as if when it comes to the soul life - we still operate in poverty, which results in poverty in body as well. So there is a split - I am a king going to heaven but I am not associated with the world and therefore I deprive myself of all material things. This is materialism - because my focus is in deprivation in the material realm. Materialism on the abundance of things is associated with worldliness. Yet for the Christian this is not the end. The end is heaven. Abundance of soul leads to a grateful life - a giving life - a life that wants to

serve and not to get. A change therefore leads to sowing and reaping - a change from a negative life style to a positive life style. How to be high and happy - this is what it is all about. It is not in what I have but who I am. It is not a lack of money but a lack of ideas. Ideas flow to a man who is walking in liberty - in true freedom - freedom to choose. We see this best when it comes to doing - there seems to be a mismatch. I want to breakthrough in all areas. My spiritual freedom must lead to freedom in my soul - to be able to choose. This choice will lead me to be free in exploring, researching, living and being a person who is free. I will seek for new heights to reach for the highest potential in me. I will not operate in a reductionistic fashion but will expand myself and be an expansionist. This is the brain shift that needs to occur - from looking to the lowest denominator to reaching for the highest nominator. So I keep stretching myself in all areas - to reach for excellence. This is dependent on my self-esteem. What I think of myself. God and I can do anything - so I will look to Him to guide me - to challenge me to new heights. I will, I believe, I can, because I am.

Confidence in self

It is confidence that is the key. I have confidence because my confidence comes from who I am in God. God has predestined me - called me, sanctified me, empowered me - so now whatever I do will blossom and flourish. It is this confidence that is transmitted to people. This then leads to new openings, success and abundance. Faith, hope, love - the 3 keys that release confidence. People desire this. If you have it then you need to share it. How? Through everyday living. You may not know everything but you are certain of your destiny. This then enables you to climb any mountain. It is this certainty that leads to the creation of events, circumstances that were not there. Wow! What a possibility. When I am in tune with God, He releases His purposes, potential, power into me and I become present, imminent, incarnational and this is what increases faith and hope till I am able to trust Him completely in all things and at all times.

Believe in yourself

Believe in yourself. This is what will count in the end. All defensive behaviour is due to a lack of belief in yourself. God has called you and entrusted you with the pearl of great price. No one is perfect. Yet in Him you are perfect. See how as you trust Him in you, you will be able to overcome. You are nothing, but He is everything. Trust His Spirit in you. He is able to overcome through you. It is not what others think but who you think you are that counts. Don't hide behind your position and status and power. Be vulnerable - this is the true path to freedom. Procrastination, analysis and false imaginations only induce fear because they are based on a false premise. Stop this. Either pray in tongues or write it down. The mind will tend to follow the negative path rather than the positive. This is induced by fear or error. You are loved and you are precious and significant in His sight - so follow His path of victory. Yes, follow the narrow path - the path that leads to everlasting joy. You are not here to serve yourself but to serve others - so live in the joy of the Lord. Ignore the weaknesses of others - laugh at your own foibles - in this way you liberate yourself. Be your own judge. Don't compare - entrust all to Him. This is the only way to complete satisfaction and contentment. God has made a path for you. One life, one wife, one destiny. Now enjoy this path. Do what He directs you to do. This is His will for you. So walk in it and rejoice. See how He will lead you each step of the way. Then share His blessings with others. Yes, a man who is determined to accept His will will forsake all others and follow Him. His ways are the best.

Leaders

Positive thinking leads to positive emotions, which leads to positive helpful behaviours. So it is transformational thinking, which will lead to positive emotions. The state of a person can be changed by changing thinking or acting as if - that is altering body posture, stance, activity. It is to alter one's habitual responses so that a continuous state of optimism, faith and leadership prevails. A leader is always on top of his environment. He is distinct. Once the environment is allowed to influence him to the extent that he looses his position or direction then he is no more a leader but a follower. A leader always leads by example. He is a leader always. Few are called to be leaders.

Resistance to change

When one has a positive, solutions focused attitude then people are freed up to be creative. This is the key to progress. But the phase of resistance needs to be worked through. There will be resistance to change in any venture. However this resistance serves to clear doubts and questions tend to strengthen ones position. So don't give up at this stage but continue to question and ask and push forward. The brain then begins to be certain. Others may voice your doubts. Again when you are solution focused then answers will emerge. No one person has all the answers - so it is as you join up with others that you become whole. Ask questions of others so that they feel respected and involved. Keep the goal in mind. Others will come through as they too see the need to be involved in the process. It is important for others to see and know that you don't have all the answers but also are knowledgeable enough. Humility, the faith position to know that you don't know it all, gives rise to hope in others to persevere and help to find the answers. The risk of being a super specialist is that you have got to get it right all the time. However this is not the name of the game - the specialist is to point the ways so that others can find the way to freedom and release. Jesus came to do just this - to walk - point the way to the Father, that, I knowing Him and His Spirit, can be led by Him to greener pastures of love, joy, peace and wholeness.

Conflict

Conflict situations always raise possibilities. I can expect conflict but it is my response that is important. I have to act as I feel for in this I openly state my position - this is true humility. Being guarded and living in the fear of repercussions is not the way to live. Lord, set me free. As a leader I will be challenged. But this challenge is good - for then I will know if what I am going through is of God or not. For the challenge enables me to question. If there is no challenge then I have to be cautious. This is good for me to know how to handle conflicts and not give up.

Areas of conflict commit it to the Lord. Don't struggle with it on your own. Conflict always polarises and paralyses you. You tend to take one position and hold on to that position even against the facts. So commit it to the Lord. Let Him deal with the situation. When you commit it to the Lord, He will work in you and those involved in the situation to change hearts and minds and positions. In the end it is not the position you hold but the relationship you preserve that is important. Arguments can cause rifts. What is said, what is not said, looks etc. It is important therefore to commit the matter to the Lord and let Him deal with the persons involved. If the Lord then works in you to change your mind, then be humble enough to do so. Remember at the end of the day the Lord is more concerned about unity than who is right. The facts of the matter do not count. Jesus went to the Cross not because He was wrong. He went to the Cross through obedience. Your preferences maybe different but what is it that leads to unity. This is what needs to hold you together. Otherwise agree to differ but still maintain unity in love. You enjoy what you have and let them enjoy what they have. The ability to handle differences and to be able to cope with ambivalence is the mark of maturity.

When you come to a place of saying, Not I but Christ, then you come to a place of total redemption. It doesn't matter what happens without - it is what happens within that matters. God has a course for you. Wait till this course is revealed to you. God will not lead you to the course in disunity but in unity.

Strategy

Strategy - the key to success. Revelation to me as I played squash with Jared. How easy it is to play the game when I know the strategy. So also in every area of my life, the only way change will occur is if my strategy is right. In exams too - the strategy is what counts- it is not knowledge but knowledge applied that counts. Don't be overwhelmed by theories and opinions - it is strategy. Strategy arises from knowledge and understanding but it is the strategy that turns the key and opens the door. In every area the problem needs to be studied and then a strategy evolved to solve it. Sometimes the problem cannot be solved but needs to be managed. Each situation, problem is unique, but a strategy usually can be found. This requires wisdom. Trusting the Lord and moving in confidence leads to new insights. **Defensive problem solving prevents strategic solutions.** One needs to be confident and move forward. It is the movement that causes the problem to shift. Fear and defence keeps one stuck with the problem. Choose the best option and start moving in faith and the problem will disappear. Most problems are related to one's perception. One's perception is related to the frame of reference. One may need a new frame of reference to understand. What is a problem for one, is not for the other. Understanding the others frame of reference will lead to the solution. Reframing the problem so that it is no more a problem. Therefore the problem was in the mind of the person till it was viewed differently.

Frames of reference

Frames of reference. Each of us uses a frame of reference. The ability to use multiple frames is what leads to maturity. Stuckness is because of the inability to see or put oneself in another's frame. "And" becomes such a liberating word. "But" is so paralysing. **So wipe out the word "but" from your vocabulary.** No ones view is the right one - what I need to know is what is the best solution in the present circumstance. If I get into a polarised position then I will not be able to see another's position. My emotions then freeze me into that position. So I need to think through multiple frames. Stuckness is due to old patterns of seeing and doing and thinking that paralyses ones ability to cope in new situations or in crisis. It is in crisis that a person is able to see how a person will cope.

I know my end and therefore I can believe that all that comes to me is to help me. Nothing will put me down because I follow the Master's voice. I will not rush but wait. When there is the impulse to rush then I must wait. It is only in quietness will I make decisions. Emotional rushes cannot be relied on. I need to step back and look at the whole picture. A man who does not count the cost cannot go that further mile. So the waiting is the time to count the cost. Once having counted the cost I know what I am doing then I can put my hands to the plough and attempt the impossible.

Problem solving

One needs to bring the facts and opinions together in a meaningful way to help in management. This means distancing myself from the position of involvement to see the larger picture and so have control over it. If I am too involved then what is in front of me clouds my vision and I lose direction and become overwhelmed by the feeling state of the patient. Involvement to empathise, distancing to observe. Helping others to do this enables them also to have control and proper perspective to enable a solution to come forth. Studying from all angles to appreciate the whole. Family work also enables me to do this - to see it from parent's point of view, children and interactional patterns. Out of this to come up with a strategy to solve the problem. Problem solving with no follow through leads to chronicity of problems. Indecisiveness and resistance to change keeps problems ongoing. The problem takes over the family. The problem then serves to distract the family from their responsibilities.

Faith overcomes fear

God gives His power to fulfil tasks at the time it is needed - not before, after. So trust in Him at all times. Don't let anxiety and worry rob you of His power. Anxiety, worry and doubt are anti-faith and trust. So empower yourself as you stir yourself in the

Holy Spirit. Doing and applying what you have learnt is what brings congruence. **The reason for a weak Christian life is due to lack of application.**
Clarified my own thoughts as I talked about it - this is the way of faith. New thoughts will flow in. So I don't have to worry - just be in faith. Faith conquers fear. This is it - faith releases the power to conquer fear. Fear is what paralyses. In any situation I have to move into a faith state to conquer my enemies - the fears, doubts, unbelief and negativity of the fleshly state of mind. It is the Holy Spirit in me that enables me to enter into a state of faith. It is faith that enabled people of God to trust God, then to trust man and so they overcame. So as I face my goals it is faith that will bring the people, resources and power to enable me to do. I need to think of the goal and new power and ability will be released to me.

Conformity

The need for conformity is so great - but conformity is not unity. We can be united even if we differ. Difference is to accept that we are all persons. The world wants to put us in a mould - so does the church. This is the reason for the splits - yet there is only one Jesus - doctrinal differences appear to separate us not unite us. It is only when we unite in Jesus that we become whole. Everything else is secondary. We can worship where we want. Maybe this is what the Lord is doing in me. I feel torn - yet I have to remain true to my belief and support others. Just as I want to be respected for my own need so also others. It is the ability to respect others positions that brings a closeness. Condemning does not work. I am becoming more aware how important the soul of man is. It is through the psyche of man that one has entrance to his spirit. God chose to work through love - there is no other way. A crippled soul whether through physical or emotional abuse is crippled - is dammed as a human being. So help in this area will release the soul to be free.
Questions are not threats but they are for more information. Good to address a question with another question for clarification. Most people have not thought it through. Faith is

a matter of belief so cannot be reasoned but the Holy Spirit is able to use your words to plant seeds.

Prosperity

Money is the root of all evil. Yes, the god of this world controls this world through money. Yes this means that I have nothing to do with it. Yet money can be a source of burden and limits my freedom to do what I want. So I need to see how I can make money my servant and not my Master. It is only when money is my master that I become its' slave and therefore will be ruled by it. My faith challenge is to break through this barrier so that money will no longer rule me. I have taken the negative approach by being restrictive rather then looking at prosperity to see how I can use money to enrich. One is a restrictive life-style, the other an abundant one. Christ came to give me an abundant lifestyle. So I change my position from a restrictive stance to a creative stance. God is the creator of all things. He came to show that there is no evil in anything except when it is abused. Sex is good. Money is good. Relationships are good. What has gone wrong is that sin has infiltrated into what is good and corrupted it. Therefore I need to change my thinking, my attitude towards these God given things to see how I can be positive and creative in these areas. In all areas of our life money controls us. Why? Because we have allowed it to and therefore it has become a necessary evil. Now the only way I can stop its control over my life is to have a lot of it. The attitude is not to have a lot of it but to be free from it's controlling influence over me. So I can live freely. In all areas Christ has come to set me free. If there is any area that is restricting me then I use faith imagination to free me from these destructive relationships and situations.

Love key to release

The key is love through faith in God. Love is an all encompassing state - it looks outward, upward and directs its' energies towards others - positive. There is healing in this love. So I need to have these positive feelings, healings and deliverances to be free to be. People are imprisoned by the system of this world. It is to live freely in this world - free from all negativity that is the true state of man. Christ came to bring this deliverance to man and this is what I want. To be free to love, serve, learn and leave a legacy. To be involved in freeing others is to free myself. Selfishness is a trap and I change my position to serve others and in this way I become a person no more imprisoned by sin and selfish attitudes but free to give. Jesus went to the Cross to pay the price to set me free. I no longer need to pay the price but enjoy His salvation full and free. So I shall be loyal to Him and His ways. Without Him I am nothing. So come Lord Jesus and set me free. It is this outward attitude of loving, giving, serving and being that releases me to be a bearer of His light. To be emotionally free is to be cut free from all emotional ties that are negative and destructive. To be emotionally whole is to like me, accept me, to be free. Hallelujah - what a salvation. God has come to give me freedom in all areas of my life. Key is to surrender to Him all the negative and receive His positive by giving myself totally to Him - total surrender so I do not belong to myself but to Him. In this is true freedom.

Programming for success

Through action the program is reinforced till I can do it automatically. When I stop thinking then I am reacting. In reaction mode I am just responding to feelings - therefore I need to be thinking of my responses - thoughts and feelings all the time. In reaction mode I am under the control of the circumstances. To be financially free is to be able to think freely and creatively. All the pressures are not over because I will still need to act responsibly. I cannot escape from a situation just because I am financially free - I cannot just behave carelessly. The principles that brought me success need to be applied continuously. As long as I am doing my best and having explored the situation from all angles I can now state the case with confidence. Other's viewpoint does not mean that I am wrong but different. It is how I manage the case that is important. I may have all the right answers but it is in good application that I know if I am effective or not.

Stop judging others

Everyone wants to project a good picture of themselves and therefore one way is to paint a poor picture of others. This is the root of negativity. A critical spirit reflects a negative spirit. A man with good self-esteem judges himself and not others. When I stop judging others then I become whole. When I project negativity to others then I will also fear a reaction. This then makes me more negative and a spiralling effect occurs which further undermines my esteem. The order of change is to stop looking for the negative in others. To concentrate on me - to be positive - to drain out the negatives and fill myself with positives. I don't depend on others for this but look to the resources within me and in God. Then as I give I shall receive good in return - love, peace, patience, joy. I am a leader so I set the tone for the interaction. If I am negative, then I set a negative tone - these then influences others who then act and react in this way. This is why it's important to have a team spirit. A team spirit looks to build others and not compete with others. This is based on positive relationships. Without a team spirit, there will be suspicion and negativity.

Opinions

Opinions are abundant based on ignorance and feeling. Feelings should always follow facts. Feelings based on opinion are dangerous. Faith on the other hand chooses to believe and then move out and the experience that follows confirms it. Facts are based on senses. Belief is based on what is written, felt and experienced.

Fixed in purpose

Success comes to the man who is prepared always. So I will wait when thoughts and feelings seem to distract me from my dream, goal, purpose, vision and mission. I will stay fixed knowing that it is in being fixed in my attitude that I will attain aptitude. This is a process of being, of living, of becoming a person in Christ. Change occurs as I stay fixed on this purpose - change to be. "I will always expect to win" - this is a false position. I should always be ready to learn - for it is in this that I will grow. I will be prepared to listen to others - for I am here to serve. It is only when I want my own way and impose it on others that I deprive myself of learning and growing. This is a mutual process. When I face difficulties and conflicts - I need to get into a positive stance to see how something good can come out of it. As the rubber hits the road - as iron hits iron - so the sparks are the process to refinement. So help me Lord. Risky living - I am and therefore I can, I will, I believe.

Pressing on

In every project, task, there is this pressure to give up - but I need to resist this pressure and press on to victory. I need to see this barrier as a wall - like Jericho's' wall that will fall. Each time I come against it by faith - the wall gets weaker. I can see it crumbling and then finally it falls and I walk through to victory - the land of plenty. So see each problem and task as a barrier to be crossed. Exams are a barrier - I keep at it, till I overcome. The exams are just a test to determine if I am prepared. So also daily problems are just a task to see how well I will be able to do the task. With faith and prayer I will empower myself in spirit and soul (state of resourcefulness) to overcome. Praying in tongues energises my spirit - now I am able to enter into a state of power, of excellence, which then sets me up higher than the barrier before me - I can see over the wall - the dream, vision, goal and I pursue the goal. I don't let the opposition, frustrations, and blocks, to diminish my vision. I press on relentlessly till I achieve the goal. This kind of challenge is important - for spiritual and emotional muscles to grow - also in exercise - it is against resistance that I feel fit. So help me Lord not to see resistance against me as a sign of defeat - failure or weakness but as a challenge - problem-solving response - solutions focused. So whatever the challenges I choose to see this as something to overcome. I am thus growing always. If I shy away from the task, then I become controlled by the environment, by the problem, situation. So the only way forward - is onward - face the problem. Use all the skills, tools, wisdom and power to overcome the problem.

Integrate your values with your goals

Anything I think or do that is in my path will work against me. So I cannot entertain anything that is out of order. This is what sin does - it blocks my path. This is what temptation does - it distracts from the course. I have chosen a course, now I have to follow this path. I have a goal and this goal is synchronous with my values and my emotion flow in line. If the parts of me are split from each other then I cannot be effective - because I am pulled in different ways. Ultimately it comes down to values. If I choose to ignore my conscience then I am victim to my lower nature. This is why Paul exhorts us to bring the body in submission to the Spirit. The Spirit must reign and rule in my life. As long as the Spirit reigns then I become a winner. When the body rules then I become a slave to the lusts of my body. So I separate myself, train and discipline myself as an athlete does to bring my body to subjection. Then once it is trained, it will submit to higher values. This is the problem that parents have been slack in training their children and so they in turn find it difficult to bring their body to subjection. It has to come from within. The Spirit gives me power to overcome but only if and when I choose to submit to the Spirit. So I am dependent on Him. Only in Him and with Him will I be able to do. So I open myself to Him. The old ways have to go and I need to be open to new ways to cope. If I keep doing things the old way then I will never be able to grow because the old ways are like old wineskins. The new wine of the Holy Spirit needs to be contained in new skins as I prepare myself - my body, soul and spirit, then the Holy Spirit can fill me. I do this through renewing my thinking - renewal of my mind > transformation.

Unblocking the flow

The water must flow. It is in allowing what is in me to flow out that enable more to flow in. This is what negativity is all about - a blocked stream. So as I begin to allow the spout to open and flow then I will experience the flow of new life through me. The staleness, putrid and smelly vapour of negativity will have an outlet to flow out of me as the fresh stream of living water is released. When the spout is blocked then what is good is also blocked. This is why involvement is so important. Jesus promised springs of living water. This water needs to be pumped up from the living stream of the Holy Spirit within you. It becomes so as I fix my mind on others then myself. Always when one is operating in faith and focus is shifted from self to the other, then the flow occurs. This is a universal principle. It is only when I am stuck in myself that the flow is stopped. I open myself up to God to receive from Him. He is waiting and anxious to fill me up. Now I need to be ready and willing to open up to others. I am blessed only as I give. Therefore since my mission is to give - I can receive from the Almighty. I cannot expect from His resources as long as I am doing everything to fulfil my own desires. It is Gods desire that results in Gods' resources being opened up to me. I have the pearl of great price within me - now it is up to me to share Him with others. I have a plan that I know will work -I share it with others. So whatever I have is to be shared - for the benefit of others. This attitude then releases others to receive for they are not threatened. I do not approach others to deprive them but to enrich them - not to condemn but to release them. This is the way to bless others. Jesus came not to condemn but to enrich. Jesus never condemned - but when people reject the message of salvation then they condemn themselves. So also when something does not work - people blame the plan - not themselves. Nothing works without hard work. It is not just the remembering of facts but the application of the same. So concentrate on application. Wisdom that is not applicable is useless. So be wise.

God is in control

God is in control - I will not let my pride, prejudice, position, envy, jealousy or anything that is mine come in the way. I release all to God. Any negativity that arises is my opportunity to let go and let God. People grow only when they are allowed to choose. Choices based on what is earthly - never satisfies. It is only that which is eternal that lasts - so all these other things are just passing by - never put confidence in them - even relationships. I cannot and do not posses anything. All I have is given to me. I need to remember this. It is these things that come in the way – Lord, liberate me - these things will be used to bless and not to cause a barrier. So I will comfort myself all the time. I will be my judge. I will then take command of the situation and purge the negatives out of me. Cleanse myself in the blood. Yes, these attitudes are hard to die - but must die. I am only free when I am able to say not I but Christ. I will give, bless and work that others may gain. Any attitude that will envy others will be broken in Jesus' name. I will not covet what belongs to others but rejoice. I will rejoice in what I have. It is this covetous spirit that splits. All I have to do is to be in tune with the Holy Spirit. Without Him I am lost - He is the pearl of great price.

Success in God

Success is the key to Gods' blessings. This success is not based on works but on faith in God to grant success. In the world success is seen and based on one's efforts whether good or bad - in the kingdom of God, success is based on trust - trusting God in all things. This means hard work, to do my part ie. working with God. A man who puts his trust in God never fails because God never fails. Each test is a stepping stone to further learning and success. Jesus death on the cross is a failure in man's eyes but a success in God's eyes and those who are saved. The Cross therefore can be seen as a negative symbol or the positive power of God. As a negative symbol it stands for pain, suffering and loss. As a positive symbol it stands for salvation and redemption - there are 2 sides - negative and positive. It is to change my attitude to be positive - to see the positive at all times that will enable me to change. There is power in seeing the positive. This is what will see you over every hurdle. You change first - then others will be effected by the change. This is slow, as old patterns take time to change. There are forces that will hinder, forces that will help. Ignore the hindering forces. Don't pay attention to these. Fix your eye on the helping forces - the new strategies, the positive forces that will enable you to overcome and not give in. Hallelujah the Holy Spirit and I will so focus on the resurrection power that the negative forces of self, world and the devil will have to give in to the positive power of God. Faith is the key to positive power > success > blessings. It is as if as you do this all negativity will be flushed out of you. Imagine victory in all situations - good and bad - hallelujah for this is your inheritance in Christ Jesus. So don't look at the situation as hopeless and don't let past experience dictate present behaviour - rather capitalise on the words and promises of Jesus for this could be the time of victorious deliverance. Hallelujah for each time the mountain is faced - it becomes smaller till you are able to conquer it.

Preparing for success

Always think of blessing others - this is a change. Need to apply these principles if they are going to be part of me. It is application that will change the old patterns. Fixed in the Holy Spirit. Leave the results to the Lord. I do my part. Don't worry about the results - that's not in my control. To do my best is in my control. Prepared for anything, but more for success. Simulating success in my imagination primes me for success. All my brain cells go into high gear - it is like a stimulant that is released to fight to win. It is this state that is required. Expect the Holy Spirit to come and lift you up and give you the knowledge and wisdom to win. This is a constant state that you need to automatically be able to put yourself in. If you feel you are going down then take a break - reenergise yourself and go back to the task. This happens when regressive patterns occur - take a break. When you reach stalemate -

take a break. When you get stuck - step back from the problem and see it from the others point of view - see the larger picture - look at the consequences - long term. In this way you are able to manoeuvre through the blocks and come up victorious.

Emotional Problems

Emotional problems are due to lack of values, hope, purpose, and meaning in life. All the hurts, traumas are self-induced or by others. There are very few that are biologically based and therefore the need is not for further complicating the matter but addressing the root of the problem - the need for love, meaning, purpose. Everything else is symptomatic of this basic problem. Where there is meaning - there is purpose - a goal. Where there is meaning nothing is insurmountable. Only if meaning is missing is life without a purpose - a goal. Most human beings drift along with the masses - structure is provided to contain the aggressive and sinful impulses, demons that seek to destroy self and others. The family and society provides this structure. However, without meaning, it is an empty shell. The shell will break under pressure because there is nothing in it to sustain the blows. Meaning is what gives the shell strength. A vulnerable self will attract pressures from without. A solid self will withstand the pressures - therefore look to God within. It is the strength within you that will sustain you in trouble times. Your future is secure in His hands so why worry.

Risky living will lead to success - for most people operate in defence and not in offence. Offensive living creates problems that have to be solved. Yet, it is just this that creates meaning and purpose.

Integrity

What I need to do is flow in integrity otherwise I will be in conflict with myself. This is what usually happens in that the conflict within is externalised. People have chosen to lie to their conscience and therefore it works against them resulting in low self-esteem. When one rejects God - one is working against one self - for the subconscious cannot accept this and therefore there is an internal conflict. We were born to worship - if this worship is neglected then we starve ourselves. Believe, faith, imagination all make me different from animals. Therefore it is important that man comes in touch with his Creator. In this there will be a connection. However man has denied the Creator because like Lucifer he wants to be in charge and therefore worships the creation rather than the Creator. This will place man in the position of God because he chooses whom he will worship. True worship is to be accorded to Creator God. This requires belief and trust. In this is true worship, unity and integrity.

Don't despair

I am being changed from within so that I can be a light. The darkness covering my soul will lift as I stay in the spirit. See how the Lord will open doors. For too long I have been satisfied in staying in the dark - not confronting and facing my fears and weaknesses. If I am to change then the wall that I have built around me has to be broken down. Your failures are part of the process. You can either withdraw or break out. This is your choice. Break out. You have been anaesthetised to a false sense of security through your job and position and wealth. You have not been living. For living is to experience life in all its' fullness. Books, knowledge etc. - talk about life but this is not living - living is the day to day experience of acting on what you know. It is so easy to be detached from all that is going on around you. It is only when you are connected to others, when you make yourself vulnerable to others that you become real. This is what I am doing in you. I am calling you out of the nest you are in. I have a treasure within you that is bursting to come out but the walls have kept you in. Mere knowledge blocks you in. The soul is missing. So don't despair but trust in Me. I have brought you and given you the desires of your heart. I want more for you than what you have now. Just move forward in faith - one day at a time. Your failures will be the stepping stones to a new place of liberty. For the failures will remind you of the fact that nothing is assured in this life. All that you have can disappear in a minute. Only faith and trust in God will last forever. So don't despair. The angels are around you. The Father will lead you. The Holy Spirit will comfort you. Do not be distracted. Just live each day to the full. See how He will change your mourning into dancing. Only the Spirit can do this. It's during these times that you are being moulded to be the person God wants you to be. The walk of faith will bring many challenges but none will be too hard for you. You are loved - this is the strongest, most solid experience that you have - the love of God so encapsulates you. Nothing is possible to break this. So bask in His love. He is strong for you. Be strong in Him. Go where the Spirit leads you. Go in His strength and in His mighty power. He has led you this far - now move forward. Don't let the forces that come against you defeat you. Press on. Keep your face firmly fixed on the goal. Exams, trials, temptations have no power over you. You are blessed - so stay fixed. It is this tenacity - this confidence that will see you through. Don't compare yourself with others. Remain fixed. Seek to grow. This is risky living - but you can because He who is in you is greater then he who is outside you, so put your faith and trust in Him. Hallelujah what a Saviour. So Lord I will trust in You. You are leading me on a different path. I know You are. I will follow - for You want me to be free to do what I want and not be boxed in by the system.

Loving self, loving others

To be responsible for my own thoughts, feelings and actions. This is maturity. I need to decide what I want. If I love myself then I will want the best for myself. If I love myself then I will want to bless others. My responses to others are just a reflection of how I feel about myself. This is why it is important to choose what I want. If I am in conflict within, confused and directionless then I will reflect this. My face will be a reflection of how I feel about myself within. I will respond to others the way I feel within. Therefore if I need to be an influence on others rather than others being an influence on me, I need to take care of myself. If I don't then I give up control to circumstances or others to control my life. When God is in control of my life then I need fear nothing because He has my best interests. If God is not in control then who is - either the selfish, egocentric, narcissistic self or the other. I therefore need to be in charge of what I think. For it is how I think that will determine how I feel and act. Feeling in the end determines action. So how I feel is important. Feelings are also linked to maturation and attitude. This is where goals come into place. A clear goal directs ones' thoughts and feelings. Then faith increases and sees the goal achieved. What is received and seen, as present now will become material reality in the future. This is so important. Hard work is good but without a vision hard work will be just like going round in circles without any direction and all you do is dig yourself deeper into a rut. So take care of yourself - body, mind and spirit. In this way you become a person that others will challenge and look up to. Accept your weaknesses, failures and trials and situation and see how accepting leads to a determined effort to overcome. Jesus looked at the Cross - struggled with it and then overcame death. So also every hurdle is a cross that needs to be overcome. The Cross is a symbol of death and victory. Death to self that seeks to spend itself on itself - victory in redirecting the forces of good on to others through the resurrection power of Jesus Christ.

Friendship

People talk to draw attention to their own needs. In this is the key to friendship. A listener is able to bless others just by tuning in to the deeper needs for love and significance. Meet these needs and you are on your way to freedom in relationships:
1. Relationship with God—Faith
2. Relationship with Man—Listening
3. Relationship with Work—Performance
4. Relationship with Self—Positive thinking
5. Relationship with God's creation—Care.

Persistence

Persistence - this is the key. It is so easy to give up when things are not going one's way. This is why one needs a clear goal - a God given goal. Then one sticks to it knowing that God is with me. Circumstances, opinions will come against you but trust in yourself and in God and that will see you through.
It is persistence that is required. Do not stop sowing. So in every area of life - there is a time for sowing - a time for reaping. Now is the time for sowing. Sow in love and you will reap the harvest in time. This is a spiritual law. What you sow, you shall reap. If you sow nothing you will reap nothing. So move out in faith. This world is more than what you see, feel and touch. There is a world beyond the physical world. Just as things do not satisfy - so also relationships will not satisfy. All areas of your life need to be satisfied. It is not wealth, popularity or friendships but life everlasting - life in Jesus that truly satisfies. He gives this through His Spirit. What I sow in the Spirit will be obtained in the Spirit. Just as Jesus forgave the sins and saw the manifestations in the flesh, so also as I sow in the Spirit - I will see the manifestations in the flesh. It will all come suddenly and this will be the evidence of things not seen. The Spirit works in you to reveal the way forward. Just trust in Him and be satisfied. You know that these other things don't really satisfy. Life, health, is in the hands of your Creator. So look to Him for your sufficiency. He is the One who will order your days here on earth. So rejoice and be glad. Do not allow envy or any other kind of disordered feeling possess you for they are destructive. Rather rejoice in the Lord always - again I say rejoice. Be bold and very courageous. The Spirit will give you the faith you require to go forward from day to day. So trust the Lord with all your heart and do not give in to the longings of the flesh.

Helping others to help themselves

The tough times will not last. God's power is released when tough times turn people into tough people.

Need to keep to a positive mind set. This is where the guarding needs to take place. So easy to become negative - then the negativity will cloud your perception and cause you to think and act in unhelpful ways. So keeping myself in the Spirit - in a positive, joyful, resourceful state of mind is essential to my productivity. This will allow me to look at other options. When I get myself into a negative state - then I become narrow and unresourceful. This narrows my options. I become fixed in my position and therefore straightjacket myself. I need therefore to be able to entertain multiple positions and roles, always looking for the best option. I cannot force people to do anything. I need to be able to motivate them to want to do it. If they want to do it, it is because they feel they have made the choice. So I need to get into a questioning mode so that they come up with the answers. Their answers then means that they have been guided to find the solutions to their problem and this means that they will learn to find solutions to their situation in future and not be dependant on others. So each conflict situation can either paralyse me or motivate me. God's purpose is to motivate me. So I choose to be motivated. This is what happens in families. People manipulate others to meet their needs - not directly but indirectly. With outsiders where the boundaries are clearer - this kind of manipulation does not take place. There is respect and therefore people behave differently - they tend to be more co-operative and resourceful. It's the clarification of boundaries at home too that is required. So the way things are done is important. There will be resistances when people feel forced to do something. I can force someone to do something but in the end I don't call forth their loyalty or respect. Therefore I need to choose. I must refrain from assuming my rights especially when it affects others. So I will depend on the Holy Spirit. I will be open to others to speak into my life. So I will change.

Problems as opportunities

It is defensiveness that kills creativity and keeps me locked in. To be free is to move in the fullness of the Spirit - to depend on God - to trust Him in every step - to convert disappointment to victory. Each disappointment I commit to the Lord and see how He changes it into victory. Victory after loss is sweeter than anything. So each time I face defeat I will look forward to see how the Lord will turn it into a victorious parade.

Without problems there are no solutions. So see problems as opportunities. Those who shy from a walk of faith will be imprisoned by their problems because they see problems as constricting and limiting them. The trials of life are what make a man. So I will not shun problems. I will face them and win. I will help others to do the same.

When I am operating from my true centre, I operate with direction. Even with difficult families - it is important to keep hope alive. One can intervene helpfully in families who are in crisis - where there is a lot of desperation - for anything that changes, then, is progress. So do not be afraid of crisis - this is opportunity for change. Change can be managed in 2 ways - either resist or change. In both cases some activity is required. To resist change is to remain in status quo. This constant pressure is required to keep people moving towards greater levels of excellence. The human tendency is to be lazy. There is only one cure for this - that is change. So if one does not motivate oneself to change then external pressures will bear upon one. So it is better to be in control and change rather than wait for external circumstances to produce a crisis to change. This is seen so many times over and over again. So choose how to live in the Holy Spirit to the full - to operate, in movement, in faith to challenge .God will give you the words you require.

Laughter

Release through laughter (emotional release). Frozen feelings can lead to distortion, conflict and wasted energy in the form of defence. This thawing of the emotional frozenness leads to a increased energy in body, mind and spirit that leads to greater strength and power in life. If one is only operating in 10% of ones' potential - then it is to release the other 90% that growth is all about. If I am frozen or stunted or limited in some aspect then that will affect all areas of my life.

Reactions

My reactions show me who I really am. So I will keep changing till I am reacting always in love. Any sinful, selfish reaction will go to the Cross and I shall rise in resurrection power. This is the only way to change. Drastic action. God will then see my heart, have mercy and bless me. God's kindness is flowing- I need to tune into it. Its what I experience inside me that I will express outside. So if I harbour jealous envious feelings and thoughts then this is what will be received at a subconscious level- or confusing messages will be received. It's the congruence between what I am and what I say and do that will transmit clear messages to the other and lead to harmony. A person who is open to bless will be a blessing and will be blessed. I will die to those self- centred, selfish and sinful desires in me and live in the resurrection power of Christ that is available to all who are born again.

The system binds

We understand the world around us through our learning but all this is partial truth. The real truth is only found in God. Any system that excludes God operates in deception or only in partial truth. I must operate in God. Yet I have been bound to operate in the system and therefore have ignored any information from outside. I am duty bound to operate within its rules. If I operate outside it then I will have transgressed the rules. So the only way I can operate freely is to be independent and not dependent on the system. This is what God has been working in me to do. I need to break out- for this is the only way I can become a source of courage to others. Others are bound as much as I am. Those who operate within their little box cannot see anything new. Sexual abuse was not considered possible till the evidence grew too big that it could not be ignored. So God is calling me to be separate. He and I can accomplish great things.
There is no gain without pain. There is no progress without a goal.

There is a certain blindness that occurs when people are wedded to one line of thought. Alternatives are not entertained. Anything that is seen as opposing that line of thinking is resisted because it is threatening. There are dangers in this, in that, part of the brain is shut off. This is what happens when people get too focused- they lose a sense of balance. Balance is essential for your whole being. Have dreams and goals but remember those are not ends in themselves. They are what you aim for but in the meanwhile continue to live a life that is full.

Goal setting

Where there is no goal then change is stifled, and energy is dissipated in conflict that does not change anything. Change must always be towards something. Otherwise the change is only in form. So have a goal. Goal setting always energises people - it brings them out of their shell - to take risks, to set new challenges, to grow, to dream, to expand, to have hopes. This is what you need. A new challenge to keep you focused in your task. To attain this goal you need to be restless. Yes restlessness is a sign that God is at work because you are not content in what you have. You want more, desire more and will attain more. So move forward in faith and believe, for God is in you and will help you. Be a risk taker and challenge the system. Know that God is with you. It is faith in God that will enable you to do this.

Goals are important to keep me on the task. Without a goal it is easy for me to relax and settle down. Once settled down it is difficult to get up. Routine and habit tends to pin me down to a set way. This is what happens in families too - children grow up but parents have settled down in their ways and resist change. Conflict. Tensions rise and world war III breaks out. The conflicts, crises are a necessary part of change. Parents and children have to work out ways to accommodate the change - set new goals and move on. There is no settling down. Unless we are on the move daily, we rot and decay. So each new day find a new challenge to move you on closer to your goal in family, work, business, and spiritual life. In every area for growth to occur - goals need to be established. Without goals there is no direction in your life. So work to establish your goals. Goal setting is a must for those who want to grow and achieve.

Investing in others

If I believe in something then I shall be able to give 100% to it. I believe in Jesus. I believe in me. I believe that God can use me to bless and provide for others. As long as I am thinking of what I can get, I will always be in debit. It is how I can bless, give, that will release faith to expect more. Investing in people is like investing in the future. Building people up to increase their potential, to instil hope will release a lot more than just doing a retail business. This is the key to the business, the system that under girds it. So too the gospel is not only to do with salvation, but the heart of the gospel is love - so love at all times. Love is able to conquer all things. Keeping to a positive outcome always releases positive energy. Negativity always stunts and frustrates because it saps energy. Negative energy is destructive. Love is positive energy that focuses in helping the individual to believe in themselves. This belief will then release a higher potential. Dreams and faith all point to higher levels. Faith in God will enable a person to exercise his belief to attain his dream. Because the dream is a goal it keeps ones eyes on the goal and not the temporary setbacks. The goal always pulls one to a higher place.

Change

We are blinded by the system we are a part of. It requires one to step outside the system to see how it is dysfunctional. So colluding with the system is so easy. When a person hears one side of the story one becomes aligned with that part and that part stands for the truth. One needs to stand on both sides to experience the difference and then one can take a middle position or a third position. It is the ability to do this that enables change to occur. A leader is able to present his views and listen to hear others and then enable the group to come to a place where a better alternative is arrived at. This requires that we think the process through. This process of thinking through involves the mind and heart. Once the heart receives the vision then the mission is driven from the heart and will be able to stand against any obstacle.

Family first

Keep your affections within limits or else you will find that it is spread too thinly. God has given you a family to love and care for. They come first. Then those outside. If you fail to feed your family you cut the source of life or your feet. So be careful not to freely give away at the expense of your family. Family comes first. So keep them in mind all the time. What ever is left can be shared with others. Don't bleed yourself. Look to the Lord for refreshment. You are part of your family so build them up. Bless others by reaching out to them.

Focusing on solutions

Remember when you are filled with good things than the negatives will become stronger because the negatives yearn for attention. Concentrating on problems is to give problems the attention. Giving problems the attention only increases their strength. Concentrating on solutions leads to a shift of thinking and perception. This is the key - faith in the solution - the Cross of Jesus. This will release resurrection power. So as you by faith look at the finished work on Calvary you receive strength to live the resurrection life by faith. All the positives of the Godhead flow into you freely. All negatives will loose their grip.

Operating in faith

Operating in faith is the one way to success. Otherwise anxiety takes over. Anxiety is the opposite of faith. Faith propels me forward to my goals. Visualising expectation, looking at it in faith and praying in tongues to purchase it. This is the walk in faith. Thoughts come into fruition when mixed with faith.

Goals enable your thoughts to have direction. Otherwise you will have a lot of thoughts but no fruit. Thoughts are like seed. They need to be captured and planted, watered, tendered, till it produces fruit. By faith each divinely inspired thought can produce fruit of its kind. So watch your thoughts, which lead to imagination. Thoughts of success and victory will result in victory. Thoughts of poverty will result in poverty. Problem focused thoughts will produce more problems. Solutions produce more solutions. Families get stuck because they want to blame others for their problems. Taking responsibility for their problems is the sure way to move the problem to a solution. Solutions are steps to success as each problem becomes a solution - each solution becomes a nugget of gold as it takes you closer to your goal. So wait in faith, wait for the solution and then move to act on it. When a problem arises, think of the solution - not the problem.

Habits

The vision must translate into the mission in the heart before it can take off. The vision must be visualised in the imagination to be keyed into the heart and mind. Then the heart will rule the mind, which then rules the thoughts that result in action, habits, attitudes and lifestyle. This is the process. Habits are formed by constant practice. Old habits will only let go when new ones come into place. Old habits can only be broken by new ones. This is why it is so important for people to practice the new habits rather than try and avoid the bad ones. Avoidance or struggle to control the bad habits only reinforces the bad habits through negative attention. So it is important not to pay attention to bad habits at all but more than this to pay attention to new habits. This habitual exercise will then translate to attitude. These are attitudes of the heart. Action is what ingrains these attitudes into the heart. Enthusiasm and strong action helps to ingrain these attitudes. Attitudes of love and faith need to be constantly focused, aroused, so that you operate all the time in this. It is so easy in a material focused world to lose sight of faith. Faith needs to be called forth. It does not happen automatically. It is an attitude of the heart, like love and hope. Whatever you have faith in will come to pass. Faith in the material is what is called materialism. Faith in God is what is called dreams. Dreams are God given positives of what can be. So when you get fired up by your dream - you begin to operate in faith till the dream is realised. Old habits, obstructions like mountains will be removed as you focus on your dream, which is beyond the mountains.

Going beyond the problems

The negatives are all covered up by a superficial front. How negatives take control of lives. I need to go beneath the front of the negatives and come and touch the real self. This is what Jesus does. He did not look at the problems. He saw the heart and called forth the real and she responded. I too want to tap into the positives of others so that they will come forth. I must not allow situations, occupation, race, religion etc. to stand in the way. We are all the same naked. It is what is in the heart that counts. Money cannot buy this. By faith I can touch the throne of God. By faith I have been reconciled, redeemed, washed, cleansed and made new. I believe, I receive, I will, to be made whole. I trust in Almighty God. I will make myself vulnerable to others so that they will be able to touch the heart of God in me. I am exposed so that God can touch others. Jesus exposed Himself even to the death on the Cross so that others could be blessed. So also I need to die daily, seek for that which is good in others - Christ in others. When I can see Christ in others then my perceptions will change. I must not be put off by the fronts. I must pass through the fronts to the real in others.

The Lord is our helper. When all others leave, God never leaves. Therefore, I will put my faith and trust in Him.

Loving others-judging their thoughts

Thoughts - how important they are. They decide how I will respond. So I need to commit all to Him - so that He will send His positive loving thoughts to me. All negativity I will direct to

the Cross. I want to be a positive influence. Whatever evil others think I want to be positive. I will always be positive to others. I will challenge their evil actions or opinions but I will always love them - knowing that God loves me. I will not judge anyone although I may judge their thoughts. Inside - they are all needy. They all need to be loved. I will love them - just as God loves me. I will maintain a positive stance at all times towards my fellow men. Even if they design evil against me - I will maintain an attitude of love at all times. In this way I will die to my own way - I will only entertain Christ's way, which is to love my enemies.
Reading is good and knowledge is good but it is only knowledge that is applied that will mean anything at all.

Love, faith and sex

Love, faith and sex are all linked together. Therefore, don't be surprised that each is stimulated in your relationships. They are closely linked together. Yet, discipline needs to be exercised for Gods law demands that you be pure and holy in your relationships. The world has forsaken God; His laws and therefore is not aware of transgressions. Sin blinds people to what is good. Good is compromised when God is ignored. Good is relative because there is no standard. God has placed a standard in mans heart and mind but since man has chosen not to acknowledge God so he has become numb in his conscience and is influenced by the norm of his sin cultured group. These norms shift depending on who are there. One's values must be internal - not external. It is these internal values that decide whether you are led from within or without. God is able to help you in your time of need when you need it. So don't be discouraged or put off. Death to the old nature is the only way to remain pure. The old nature will pollute all relationships and this is what consumes the mind of the world as depicted in movies, plays etc. People get an indirect satisfaction as they participate in this ritual of play-acting. It is powerful and influences the mind. All relationships in movies end up in a sexual act. So sex under girds all relationships and is seen as normal. However, a man with values does not succumb to these influences but stands. He acknowledges his own fleshly needs but he does not give in to them. It is what you think and allow to think in your quiet time that determines what you will do in the world. So stay close to the Lord. Purify yourself and your relationship in the blood. Look at life with eternity in mind - not short term but long term view and walk in the immediate with that in mind. The past is gone, forgiven, forgotten. Today is to be lived and change occurs as I choose to live today - each moment in righteousness. As I look to God, He will grant me all that I need to know and the strength to do, to live a life of favour in His sight.

Powerful change induction

Christ's words must be associated with strong imaging for the message to get through. Habits are broken through in the same way. Bad habits die hard. Change of attitude needs a similar impact. Goals - dreams are motivating forces that drive one to excellence. It is the goal that is important - everything else is just part of the process. If one has a goal that is powerful enough then one can achieve anything. All obstacles will diminish when the goal is big enough. The goal must synchronise with one's ethos and be congruent in mind and heart. Flowing in unison is important. If anything does not flow then whatever is obstructive diminishes the power to reach the goal. In marriage the parties must pull together otherwise a lot of energy is dissipated. This is part of the process. Your partner on your side is important in reaching the goal. So be positive. Positive attitude crosses out the negative. The positive is more powerful than the negative. So in a negative situation bring in the positive. This is the only way forward. The positive power of God is at work in you. Only when you love it comes across and convicts and challenges others. So also only speak when you can agree. Do not speak when you can't - it is a waste of time. Lying is a waste of time - wastes internal resources. Stick to that which achieves your goals. You have a goal - a plan - a destiny. Just follow Gods leading as you keep the goal in mind.

Love gives and gives

Love must come first before change can occur. Love is communicated through relationships. Without a relationship no change can occur. When people are loved, they want to do. They do not have to be told to do. Loves response is to give. God gave His only begotten Son. When the Holy Spirit was given to you - you received Him. Now He abides in you and you abide in Him. When He is called, He responds in love. It is His love that you feel. So as you give, you too will be blessed. Don't respond to human love that is conditional. God's love is unconditional. It gives regardless. But this love needs to be shared. Only then will love be given. That is why whenever you share you feel good.
Love is an act of my will. I choose to love. I choose not to give in to my lower nature. It is in the midst of negativity that I need to give even more.
Every opportunity to give is an opportunity to love.
The negativity in you and in others can only be healed through love - Jesus love - love that abides - never changes - is there all the time - agape love is what will change the world. It is this kind of love that does not see the external but the internal and brings forth the best in others. When you feel selfish and fleshly - call on this love. Let this love of God nourish and feed you till you are filled to share it with others. It is only through faith that you can tap into this resource. Love knows no limits. It just continues to give. God's love demands a response. Why? Because love always has a response. Love cannot be sustained without a response. It is only as I respond that God's love is released to me. I control the amount of love I experience. If I do not respond then I deprive myself of Gods love. I can tap into God's love only when I come to Him in emptiness - so that He can fill me. God's love is a response. Gods love is available freely to all but it is only as I respond that I am touched. So God asks for an active involvement - my will must be submitted to Him - to call on Him - to respond to Him. I call on His name and He responds in love. It is as I see the negativity and emptiness of my soul that I cry out to Him. He

responds in love to my cry. Nothing can separate me from God's love. God's love is eternal - limitless. God's love can break through any heart. As God's people plead in prayer - this is love - power is released in the spirituals - believe, receive and release by faith. By faith I listen to the rhema word of God - I receive it - then I release it. It is the rhema word of God that heals, restores and recreates.

Giving as sowing

Giving must be a way of life for me. I cannot but give. It is when I stop giving that I become stale. So one of the indicators of staleness is that I have withdrawn into myself and have stopped giving. Giving must be a joy. I must see giving as sowing. Giving by helping, encouraging, touching, looking, and supporting. Always to be someone who looks at ways to give so that others maybe blessed. This is a reversal of a life of withholding, to faith and abundance. So the key to abundance is a servant attitude that seeks to serve and to give which releases blessings from God through others. As I choose to do this daily then others will be encouraged to do the same. I must lead in this area. Giving is to die to the flesh. The flesh seeks to keep, to indulge the self in its own enjoyment. The Spirit seeks to give. The attitude of the Spirit is always to encourage and to give. It is the Christ like attitude that finally gets through to the people. It is the manifestations of the Spirit - gifts and fruits that lead people to seek for more of the Spirit. So I must not pretend that I have anything. What I have is from God. He can give and He can take away. Just as the body without the spirit is dead, so I am dead without the Spirit of God in me. As long as I seek to bless I don't lose anything. I lose only what I hold on to tightly. So I must continue to keep this attitude in mind. That all I have is from God and I store up treasure in heaven as I choose to give. The attitudes of men do not change quickly. However the Spirit in you will touch them. This is what will change them. God is working in you so that as you give yourself completely to Him, He will change you to touch others.

Childhood experiences

My childhood experiences are also seen in perspective. Although of significance, they can now be tolerated more effectively. Childhood experiences therefore leave a significant mark because of their significance. Those experiences are keyed into the mind and it is only as an adult that those experiences can be truly integrated within the matrix of a larger experience of life. When an adult experiences what was experienced as a child then childhood feelings - suppressed are re-experienced as an adult. The adult then heals through perspective. If those feelings are suppressed then healing cannot take place and in a crisis those fears are re-experienced as overwhelming.

Significance and love

A mans basic need is for significance - while a women's need is for love. It is the ability to meet these needs that leads to a harmonious relationship. If those needs are not understood then any problem becomes a battlefield to meet those needs through control. A person needs to control only because he feels insecure. He feels insecure because his needs are not met. In Christ all our needs are met and I tap into His power source and love source. Love is needed to nurture me to health. Power is needed to enable me to achieve. So also love produces fruit - and power releases gifts. The two must go together. Emphasis in either gives rise to a limited life. Just as there is right and left brain activity - so also in life there are two activities that need to go hand in hand. Emotion and knowledge must go together. This is why some are more effective communicators than others. A purely intellectual approach is dry - and a purely emotional one can be equally draining. The key is to bring balance - to access both areas of the brain. In the Spirit there is perfect balance - so when you seek to be filled - any need for significance and love is met - the gifts and fruits are released so that you can share this with others. When you are not filled then you can't fill others.

So you are filled to fill others - to share His love with others. This is the only way. For this to occur, you must be prepared to let go of your life and be filled with God's life. This is the spiritual exchange - the heart transplant that occurs. This is what is called a paradigm shift. When you can be open and freed from your old self - then you are totally free. You don't have to spend energy in tuning your old self for it cannot be tuned – it only can be defended against. In Christ the old self is crucified. The new self is born again. The old self cannot be born again but it will be destroyed forever in death. The new self lives on forever. As you move out in faith then you will walk and operate in the Spirit - in the new self - in the new life.

Difference and beauty

Difference is what creates beauty. I need to synergise with difference. I need to be committed to what I believe. The difference can be for separation or for creative solution. To conform is what the general population seeks for - conform and unite. However difference enables others to say and do, to create a third alternative. This is more difficult because it disturbs the norm and causes confusion and conflict but this is necessary for any creative process. It is only a truly independent, secure person who can enter into being different. Others just conform. No deal, is an option - which says, "I will not bend to pressure, I have my own principles and those principles I will stand by because I depend on this for my integrity."
The facts are just the maps - not the territory. The territory maybe different because people are different. Questions do respect people and lead them to find answers for themselves. It's better than giving answers. In this process you also learn.
Emotions are aroused that are like bullets that fire off its deadly fire. Possessiveness is a kind of curse. We are born individuals. We grow in a family, which suppresses our emotions and individuality. So we feel unworthy and unrecognised. Some fight this by withdrawing from others and keep others at a distance. But then this causes or arouses

loneliness in us. We feel alone and so try and create new relationships, which arouse old fears, and this needs to be worked through. This mostly occurs in therapy and in close healthy relationships. When one partner is healthy then there is chance for the other to grow through acceptance. When both are needy then the manipulations occur. So it is your responsibility not to be challenged by the emotions and give in but to stand on what you believe. You must foster interdependence otherwise the old patterns will be repeated. You need to lead by fostering what is good and healthy and in this process a new pattern will emerge.

Prayer and imagination

Prayer is the vital link between God and man. There is no other way. Imagination is a vehicle to aid in communication with God. Where there is no imagination there is no ability to ascend above the senses. Imagination is the faculty of the mind to transcend the senses - to be able to abstract and extract the information from the senses. To be able to deduce and reason and come up with new ideas. God uses your imagination to enable you to know His heart. It is with the imagination that you see the possibilities beyond the material. Your imagination gives you the ability to experience in your flesh what is not possible with your senses. Your senses are limited to the five channels. Your imagination is limitless. Those who are free are able to imagine and so advance beyond the limits of their senses. This is the reason for masses of books, ideas and proposals. It takes an imaginative writer to write fiction. Lord, fire up my imagination. Living is marred because you dread the thoughts, feelings and images aroused by your imagination. Imagination is to do with images. These images are translated into words. These words then inform the mind. Your understanding comes from your capacity to put into words the thoughts, images, ideas, feelings and experiences. All these need to be verbalised. God will confirm what is of Him. Don't reject any of these ideas - God put them there. You belong to God and you have committed all things to Him. So believe that He will see you through. Never mind what you do - your end is assured. So live with the end in mind. The suffering, trials and pressures are all temporary. The body will decay and die, but your spirit will live on. So charge your spirit with the Spirit of God within you. Be bold that you are in the Kingdom of God. The angels of heaven guard you. You are loved. So rejoice at all times. It is like you are a millionaire for your wealth is in heaven - stored up forever where moth and rust cannot destroy. Abba, Father is looking after you. So humbly give yourself to Him and look to Him for all your needs. He will direct your paths - go act in this confidence to live life to the full, knowing that His will, will be done. He is the one in control - so rejoice.

Self centred to other centred

Moving on from a position of using others for ones own pleasure to one of service. This shift occurs as I recognise that it is in blessing others that I am blessed. As long as I am the centre then others will feel used. In the Holy Spirit I become a server - I am filled in His love to serve. I no longer operate to serve myself - to glorify myself but I live for another. I subjugate my own needs for the needs of the other. I lead by example. I don't expect from others what I myself don't give. I choose to lead by example. This is a shift from being I centred, to other centred. This is the only way to grow and break out of the me position. I deprive myself and live in poverty as long as I live for myself. It is when I reach out and begin to look to others and see their needs that I become a vessel of beauty. The beauty of Jesus is seen in His total submission to the Father - to do His will. So also it is as you submit to Him that He fills you to fill others. God blesses you and gives you victory only so that you can be a source of encouragement, love and power to others. It is in service to others that you become a living life-wire for Him. God sees your heart - now submit to Him. You can do nothing without Him. Don't get tangled in the affairs of men or the world - rather live simply - rejoicing in His abundance to you. He is in you and each day He gives to you, to enjoy all things. So rejoice that eternity is your life span - so there is no need or cause for you to worry or to fear.

Just trust the One who is in you. He will lead you and guide you. Your chief concern is to communicate Jesus to others. In your job, family, church, outside, it is Jesus that needs to smile, touch and be felt.

Praying in tongues

Praying in tongues - this is the way to meet the needs of others through the Spirit. The Holy Spirit will pray through you and then reveal the answers to your conscious mind. In praying in tongues you are submitting the situation, feeling, temptation, thought, to Him, who then gives you the power to overcome. So you can overcome all things. The negative is just the opportunity to prove Christ is in you. Repent of your selfish reactions and then look to Him to shine through you. This is the marvellous transformation that will take place as you trust in Him. Jesus is the One who counts you as present - there is no other way. Each one is accountable - so don't dismiss your weaknesses and sins through looking for them in others. Rather entrust them to Christ and the demon, sins and lusts will not harass you, but will let you go and He will shine through you.

The Lord is my Shepherd

The Lord is my Shepherd I shall not want. This is it - I will never want as long as the Lord is my Shepherd. He cares for me. He gives to me abundantly. I must learn to be content in what I have. I live to serve. I choose to let go of my own preferences. I have the Lord and He is all that matters. I choose to give and to serve - for in this, is there joy. As long as I hold on to what I have - I starve and die. It is in giving that I find my chief joy. Giving to my wife and children. To look at ways to bless them. God has given me so much. Now I want to do my best for Him. It is in serving Him that I feel blessed. I open myself to others. I become vulnerable so that the death I die to self will bring blessing to others. It is in dying to self and giving to God that there is peace and joy. As long as I live for myself then I become another number. God has a purpose for me. I need to live each day in the fullness of His Spirit.

Empowered from within

The power of the indwelling of Jesus is what makes the difference between a saint and a sinner. Jesus has come to liberate the sinner from the curse of the flesh. Yet man wishes to gain his own salvation through the works of the flesh. The Spirit dwells in you to enable you to live a victorious life. Don't put yourself down - it's your perceptions and your own thinking that puts you down. Think big, best and excellent. Think in terms of what you know is best. Be vulnerable. Learn through being a servant. It is sin that keeps man bound to his sin. Learning liberates. Knowledge is good but it is only knowledge applied that brings change. So don't be discouraged when you don't remember things - this is because it is not applied knowledge. Let the Spirit bring to your remembrance the things you need to know. As you do so He will make it part of your life. Yes, you are the instrument - so strive for excellence. God has called you to be - you are the best you can be today - now live in this and do your best. It is not what you don't know but do know that is important. What you don't know is of no use. So seek to understand and learn to know. Now operate in the knowledge that you do know. Do not compare with others. Others are where they are. Move from a position of independence and competition to interdependence and cooperation. This is a paradigm shift. You have to set the example. As you choose to lead by serving, by encouraging and supporting others in their endeavours - then you become a saint. This is what it is all about - Jesus came to serve so that He could save many. God is calling you to be separate so that you can be filled in Him to be a blessing to others. You cannot operate freely as long as you are fearful of others. Different aspects of the problem, situation, needs to be looked at. No one is perfect. Everyone only knows in part. Your part is to share what you know. The textbooks will say a lot of things but you need to choose from the different options or influences or approaches to fit the approach to the problem that will solve the problem. This needs action.

Faith in action

It is action that produces change. Sometimes understanding leads to action but many times understanding leads to no action. This is because man tends to rationalise. Jesus has called us to walk by faith. This is to step out and not seek to understand everything before you take action. Faith calls for action. Faith without action is dead. So listen and wait on God - He is able to do because he lives in you. So do not despair. All that you are going through will serve to strengthen you. Don't compare - you are the vessel of great price - to live each day to serve and to bless as a representative of Jesus Christ.

Depending on God for all things

Life is in giving. God gave and He set the example. Christ emptied Himself of all things - so that He could depend on His Father for all things. So also for you, the same plan of depending on the Father for all things. The material world only satisfies the body and your senses. The deep things of the spirit, soul cannot be satisfied with things. Like has to minister to like. The pursuit of wealth will not satisfy the needs of your soul and spirit. This is the reason for the high suicide rate and accidents. People need love. People need others to acknowledge them. In this age of computer and information explosion everyone is a number. It is only those who resist from joining the rat race and step back to follow the straight and narrow way, that will attain true happiness. True happiness is a state of mind. This comes through absolute renunciation of the things of the flesh and a coveting for the things of the Spirit. This is true abundance, godliness and contentment.

Hitting rock bottom

No more impressions to live up to - especially the impressions of others. Having hit rock bottom you are now able to climb the ladder of God. Before this you were still holding on to your fantasies of who you are rather than holding on to God who supplies all things. Just as an alcoholic needs to hit rock bottom so also you. You suddenly realised that the bottom is the rock. Your fears subside for you now know that your feet are on the Rock of Ages. He is there holding you. You now do not live on the basis of your fantasies or the opinions of others. You are free to be yourself. Hallelujah. So also it is at the point of no return that change can occur for the better. As long as you are holding on to some flimsy straw of what you have or earned - you cannot change. What you hold on to will keep you bound to the flesh or the world. Only complete surrender and consecration for Gods service matters. There is no other way. You are free to be used of God for His service. Now you can relate with others freely - blemishes and all because your life is in God and empowered by God. He is the One who will see you through each day from victory to victory.

Two competing forces

Two competing forces occupy our time. One is the force to do with daily life, the other to do with our fantasy life. They are both valid experiences but one is only a fantasy although the mind cannot differentiate between the two. However, I can choose which I will spend my time on. Fantasy life can be an escape from the real pressures of life. One who lacks fantasy is a robot and lacks feeling and imagination and creativity and such kinds can be seen in autistic persons who are fixated on routines and numbers and things. Their lack of a fantasy life deprives them of any joy in the creative - they operate more by rote - this maybe connected to their difficulties in empathy and feeling for others and for themselves as persons. This will interfere with their ability to relate with others. Their intercourse is strained and robotic and does not have the feel of mutuality or reciprocation.

Total dependence on God

Emptied of oneself - total dependence on God - this is the

place of perfect rest. I am in Him - I am loved and I rest in Him. The opposition increases as I choose to commit all to Him. The temptation is to compromise. There is no solution in compromise. God is light and there is no darkness in Him. To fight evil, the only way is to shine as the light. Allowing darkness to infiltrate the light is to darken the light. The light must extinguish the darkness. So do not be surprised by the opposing forces that will rise to bring you down. Stay in the light - pray in tongues - focus on Jesus and the temptation will flee from you. Keep your eyes on what you have and God will bless you. Seek to be at peace with everyone especially the one who irritates and troubles you the most. He/she has been placed there for a purpose - just like Judas was to Jesus. Ultimately the evil projected into you will boomerang on to the one who assails you. This is what happens to those who conspire to bring evil upon you. The light within you will extinguish the darkness. Difference brings out the light more. Difference shows up the dark areas that need to be brought to light. It is always like this. If you are only comfortable with the people who are alike then no growth occurs. Growth is stultified. Just as a caterpillar has to break through the cocoon to fly as a butterfly - so you need to struggle through the difference. Jesus was spat on, ridiculed, and outcast, because He chose to walk in the light. Walk in humility. You won't be right all the time. Be vulnerable for in this way you will find strength.

Maturity

Maturity comes through the process of dealing with the negatives in life. The positives don't make a man. It is only the negatives that will strengthen you to withstand in the day of temptation. It is just like a child who is learning to walk. It is the falls that enable the child to walk - to strengthen its legs and balance. Then he goes on to attempt the bike and other skills. Yet, in all of life it is balance that leads to moving forward. Without balance you get stuck in one extreme or other. The whole being needs to move in balance. Emphasis on one aspect either will get you stuck in the mud or move away from the target. So seek to see opposite points of view - seek to hear from the receiver and the giver. Seek to understand the other point of view. Then bring the whole together. In this way you will move. You will be stroking the right and left brain - the pros and cons. It is not whether your idea is the only one but to look at it from all points and then to discover the direction. To hear the parents view and the child's view - to resolve conflicts through understanding and not through who wins. This is the only way forward. This is the crux of management. Leadership is to see from a different vantagepoint into the future. The leader has to keep his vision high to enable the troops to know the direction of the ship. The captain has to set the course. The team works towards achieving the goal. Without a goal, a plan, a vision the mission will fail. It is not enough to do the daily work. There needs to be a proactive move to engage in work that will break into new ground.

Connecting behaviours and emotions

A problem solving approach is one way to tackle the issues confronting a person. However, the problem maybe behaviours that constitutes a disorder. So treating the disorder should remedy the behaviours. Just like unlove could produce a lot of negative behaviours. So love will encourage positive behaviours. So solutions are in effect the opposite of the presenting problems. If problems present the negative of a person - solutions present the positive. If stealing is due to lack of self-esteem - then increasing responsibility has the effect of increasing confidence and self-esteem and eliminates stealing behaviour. The emotion is the motivating force to elicit the behaviours. So if there are a lot of negative behaviours - it is due to negative emotions. One feeds the other. It is automatic. Change comes from changing or addressing both. Putting on positive behaviour over negative emotion is just window dressing. So choose to be positive and receive the love of God into you, so that your behaviours are positive and caring.

Emotional independence

Let others be happy in what they do. This separation and independence is healthy. You need this to appreciate others. Lack of independence leads to lack of appreciation for the needs of others. Dependence leads to manipulation. It only sees the needs of others in the context of ones own needs. Emotional independence is crucial to healthy relationships. So when you see yourself regressing - step back and see what is happening. Stay centred in you and whatever the forces from without, in the centre, you will not be moved. You will remain firm and steady, unmovable as a rock - your life centred on the Rock and in the Rock, you will never have to move, for He who is within you never changes. His love is always available to you. Draw from Him and be strong. Hallelujah the attacks from without are a source or opportunity to be strong and to be able to stand in the midst of trouble - so rejoice and be glad.

SPIRITUAL INSIGHTS

The revelations here, I have received, as I have waited on the Lord to reveal His mind to me.

God's love

Love is the key to abiding in the light of Christ. There is no darkness in love. Love seeks the best in others. Love is wholesome. Love never thinks or sees the negatives in others but only the positives. Love always encourages and supports. It is not possessive. It serves. In such an atmosphere only good can thrive. All darkness will disappear as Christ's light shines brighter in you. All the fears that thrive in darkness will melt away. All hatred, jealousy and every other vice will be uprooted from your heart for love will prevail.
So choose to love today. Be tolerant with the differences of others. Strive to serve others and not to lord it over them. Be vulnerable for it is in this way that you become lovable. A proud man keeps a stiff upper lip and does not allow himself to be vulnerable. He protects himself but in the process loses out on the good things of life.
Christ is in you. It's as you acknowledge His presence within you and live in Him that you will grow in righteousness and fruitfulness. This is a faith position and all you need to do is to fix your heart and mind in Him and He will shine through you. When evil appears so close at hand continue to maintain your faith position and see your enemies flee.
Only in Him are you safe. No other defence is sufficient. Defence only serves to keep you in your prison. So be bold and let Him take charge of you. Listen to Him and all other voices will come and go. Be secure in His love. He loves you. His love is real and He will keep you at all times and see you through all times-good and bad. Your confidence must come from who you are in Him and not in yourself. You are nothing in yourself but you are a prince, a king, and a son in Him. Knowing this you need to submit all to Him so that His light will shine

through you and bring all the barriers down. He is the beginning and the end. There is no one like Him. He is the Alpha and the Omega. In Him you abide and in Him will be your joy and comfort.

His presence in you is your hope of glory. It is His presence that makes you want to live. Nothing else matters. You can do what you like and live life freely because you know that nothing that happens to you can separate you from His love. Now you choose to love because you know Him who is from the beginning. He loves you eternally. There is no one who loves you like He does. His love is real. You can feel it, pass it on to others. It is not just a feeling. It is deeper than a feeling - it's like joy that is deeper than happiness. So deep that you are never empty. So whatever happens - know His love deep within you, which will insulate you from all the negativity in the world. His love will, so fill you, so you will be able to smile at all times. No problem or predicament will upset you because His love protects you. You know that like Daniel in the lion's den that you have nothing to fear for you have overcome the greatest fear - the fear of death. All other fears - rejection, loneliness, and isolation are nothing compared to the fear of death. Now you have the pearl of great price - so you can live and love and be a person totally free to be a light source to others who can experience the love, warmth and hope of God Almighty. God's love is so real that it banishes all fear and unbelief. The enemy of your soul will try and corrupt through images to experience a distortion of true love - never give into the superficial for the real. When you have the real then the sounds and sights of this world just grow dim and all you desire is to be close to Him - to know Him is to love Him. This is the message of the gospel. Jesus Christ came, as a man to prove to the world that God the Father loves the world. His love is the key to all other hopes and dreams. Without the knowledge of His love, there is nothing that satisfies. Everything else is temporary - there is no meaning in anything without the knowledge of His great love. So be strong and very courageous as you step out to change the world from a negative, poverty stricken mind set - to a positive, abundant mind set.

So remain fixed in Him. Everything around you may change but as long as you are fixed in His love, you will need to fear nothing. Do not be afraid to ask and discuss for in this way you clear your thoughts and also are able to see more clearly. Defence cages you in. It's better to be honest and open then defensive and closed. It's openness that will lead to openness.

Only a man who is afraid and self -possessed needs to plan every move. A man who is dispossessed lives each moment in His strength and is alive and not dead. God's love is not soft. God loves with a wholeness that no one knows in the flesh. His love is beyond comprehension because it is so large, so wide, so high and so big. Yet we know something of Gods' love in His Son. Jesus did not come to condemn. Yet He came that we may be set free from the power of sin through His death. He died that I may live. What more can love do. I deserve to die - yet He died in my place. So His life is a gift to me - not to be earned but received by faith. Now I am free to enjoy this new life, everyday, as I trust in Him. His love envelops me - gives me the joy hope and will to love and live, not in the strength of my own life, but His life. This is the gospel.

The sooner I stop striving and start living the more I will enjoy His life within. All His resources are available to me. Jesus came to liberate me from self-control ie. trying to live my life as if I was in charge. This is a fantasy, a lie, short lived, destined to fail, and a delusion. Yet many continue to live for the now. All I have will be of no use to me when I die. What is the legacy I want to leave behind - things that are of no use or love, joy and peace in the Holy Spirit? It's only as I die just as Jesus died that His resurrection power is released to me to love and to be a living, powerful witness to His name. It's only as I realise that I am, only because He is, that I become one with Him and in Him, just as He is in the Father. It is as He becomes integrated into all areas of my life - as He is acknowledged as Lord of my life that I become integrated as a person - that I become one in Him. I am whole in Him, to be a shining light in a dark and fallen world. Living is different from being a robot following and doing. Living is a vital, vibrant and valid experience that comes from walking in the spirit - it is a spirit led life. This kind of life is only possible for a person who has experienced Gods' love, is committed to Jesus and is open and vulnerable to others. This kind of life is not for those who are self-sufficient, proud and live by sight and not by faith.

The knowledge of God's love is the beginning of wisdom. His love will change your perception of others and situations to enable you to see from His point of view - this is true wisdom. Jesus always tried to see it from His Fathers point of view. He had fore knowledge and was able to speak to situations. He exercised discipline, discernment and knew the heart of man. He spoke to the heart of man. He did not speak to superficial aspects of man but to the deep longings and needs of man. In this way He spoke to the unconscious. The unconscious received the message, was healed and a new man was born. So also Gods love penetrates into the depths of your being to release you into wholeness. His love is real and therefore can be experienced. His love will enable you to be real for it will well up from within you. His love will dispel all fear of man and what he can do to you. His love will deliver you from your past. His love will bring contentment. You will be so content in His love that nothing else will matter but to serve Him with all your heart.

It's His love that needs to be received in your heart. His love is healing and life. Everything else is empty promise - no depth, no life everlasting. His love is eternal. God's love will enable you to stand anything. It's in relationships that His love will be experienced. Just as God loves through your relationship with His Son so also His love is expressed through relationships with others.

God is above the systems and ideas of man. When man is submitted to Him then he will be able to imitate the real that is above what is seen. This produces life and health. God's word is just a symbol of what is real. His word becomes real and you are able to tap into the real as it is received by faith. Faith is the unseen channel for receiving the good things from heaven. So be bold and be strong and do not fear the evil one. He is only able to influence you if you give him permission to do so by submitting to the lusts of your flesh.

The Lord is good and His mercies endure forever. He is the Alpha and Omega-the one eternal God and from Him comes all good things. He gives to His children the desires of their heart. He withholds nothing from them. He is their rock and their salvation. He is always there and never takes His eyes off His children. His eye is always on His child. This is the Father heart of God. He is the One who is present to the one whose eyes are on Him. It's through faith that the child receives and knows His Father. It is through Him that he receives all that he needs-love, joy, peace and abundance. The Father lavishes His child with abundance. There is no lack on the part of the Father. The lack is on the part of the child who looks elsewhere for his needs then to his Father. The devil will try and rob the child of his inheritance. The forces of evil are at work where good is. The only way to remain in and under the influence of good is to abide in Him. There is no other way. Several are the influences from without but it is the child that trusts that will know His peace in all circumstances. There is no other way to overcome. A child who seeks his Father's will, will know and therefore do because perfect love has captured his heart. Love that is unconditional is able to receive and give much. So determine in your heart to always love.

Take hold of any and every negative thought and word and direct it to the Cross. Only what is positive should remain and fill your life. God is positive and He is good. He, who abides in Him and knows Him, knows that He is all righteous and pure and holy and there is no evil in Him. It is only the negative and fallen image of man that leads to distortion of the truth. Perfect love casts out all fear. There is no fear in love. Love conquers all. So now receive His love. Live in the positive power of love. Let love drive out all fear and negativity from you. Entrust all to Him-He is the keeper of your soul. Live like a servant. Do not shrink away from the evil around you. Learn to abide in the good in you-Christ Himself. Know that He will impart to you what you need to know and say. Be careful that no evil thought or feeling takes over you. If it does be sure to resist and renounce for the evil is not of Him but of self or another.

So in this way stay pure at all times. Do not be taken up by material issues.

Submit all to Him. He will turn those around who rebel and

resist Him. Pray much that the forces of evil shall not prevail. Always stand for righteousness. Aim for the best. Treat your body and its desires severely that you may not lower your standards. Live always to the glory of His name. Confess the weaknesses of the body. Serve at all times and His power will be released to you to overcome in all circumstances.

Whatever possesses a man will direct and lead him. If a man is possessed by the lusts of the flesh then these lusts will control him. So be careful that at all times only the Holy Spirit controls you. Commit all things in prayer to Him and do not allow your own desires to control you and others. What is committed to Him, He will take and protect and possess. You own nothing for you belong to Him. Yet you have all things for you belong to Him.

So be free and enjoy all things. A man who is crucified has lost all interest in the world and the things of the world. He is tuned into God who is above the heavens and the earth. Nothing can take the place of God in his life. God is all in all. A man who is true to himself and to others will be known and will attempt great things and achieves great things for he goes out knowing that God is with him.

Listen to God. This is the only way you will grow. Otherwise you will just go round in circles. You can only operate in the knowledge and information you have. The more information you have the more able you become to decide on the best option. The less information you have, the less options are available to you. So do not be restricted but seek and you will find. Ask others but most of all seek for the wisdom from above.

A lot of information appears good but does not have any substance. Only knowledge that is based on the Truth will last. All else will fade away with the test of time. Only the knowledge of God will bring a person to a place of confidence in Him. He is the eternal One - the everlasting one. In Him there is no change. All else will change and decay because all else is created.

He is the Creator and He never changes for He is the ultimate. When you are tuned into Him, you receive His character - you grow to be like Him.

This is why you should not close your mind but be open to others to listen and to be challenged and in this way you will grow to know and be strong.
Release your inner child today to be free and to grow. Do not be bound by anything. He will cover you and will guide you. Seek for the best and you will find the best.
It is into Him - the eternal God that you need to be in tune to. For when you are in tune with Him then you become like Him. He is ever seeking to influence you. But He can only have influence into your life as you tune into Him. His life-giving Spirit will so infuse you with His power and life that you will desire to live only in Him. The forces of evil, of destruction and decay work against you to pull you down. But His power is available to give you life. So the balance of what influences you depends on you. The more you abide in Him and seek His mind in all things - the more you become like Him.

Live in the now

Therefore do not be influenced by all the attractions and influences of your senses but learn to intuit the real - the eternal now - the being who is God manifested in the person of Jesus Christ. The Holy Spirit will make Him known to you. Be confident in the knowledge that He is with you and is guiding you. Lean on Him when you feel yourself going into defence. Live each day as if you are alive from the dead. Live in the now. Your past is in Him-consumed in Him-washed, cleansed and restored in Him. Your future is in Him - so you need have no fear of the past-of what it can do to you-nor of the future - of what lies ahead. You just need to live in the now and enjoy every moment of it - knowing that He is in control of your life.
Let this knowledge and assurance so fill you that you will walk with your head high but always being aware of your vulnerable state.

In Christ

Jesus is the bridge on whom you should walk. For when He is Lord then He will direct the way you should go. You walked knowing not where you were going. Yet this is not what God has called you to. God has called you to live each day as if it is the last day on earth. He wants to exude His beauty and life through you. This is His purpose for each one of His children. All your needs are met in Him. He just wants you to enjoy each day He gives to you. So be free from all that will rob you of this inheritance. Don't hold on to past resentments, failures and guilt. Free yourself today from these locusts that feed on you. Fill yourself with His goodness, righteousness and love. You are complete in Him. You have a new identity - live and move in it. Don't exert yourself on others but rather knowing who you are in Christ - learn how to serve others in the Spirit of Christ.

Time and money can be like gods that we worship and submit to. These are worshipped in a materialistic age. When a person is freed from looking for the praises of men, then one is freed to live and speak for God. Fighting evil means suffering in the flesh.

Think always in terms of solutions. Jesus is the only source of freedom. Being in Christ means all else has to bow to Him in you. Being in Christ means exercising His authority, humility and power. Overcome all anxiety and care by living as one who is bound for heaven. Let the vision of lost souls preoccupied with other things, wandering in a desert land filled with illusions of liberty, fulfilment and satisfaction, drive you to your knees in prayer for the salvation of souls. Only such a heart can love like Christ. If your desire is not for lost souls, then your love will be superficial. People are taken up so much by their diseased, hurt, rejected selves, that they find ways to keep themselves unconscious of their real selves. Your real self is hid in Christ. The dead man in Christ has no rights but to love and serve his fellow beings. A man who is prepared to give up all for God is the man who will be able to stand amongst the people and lead them.

The temptations of the flesh cloud the soul and cripple its life. Decisions have to be made, but it is the process of decision making that is important.

The body will always reflect the state of the mind; for example, death wish leads to cancer. It is what is within the person that matters. Sow the seeds of the Spirit by expressing the fruits of the Spirit.

The cross is the only way from deliverance from self. Every other way is an illusion. In Christ, you are crucified. In Christ you are risen from the dead. Now go and serve Him in others.

Rest in Christ

You have been called to be light and salt. So be sure to be that as you submit yourself to Him. The power of God will fill you and you will move in His authority to slay all who will walk in darkness. Christ came to deliver the captives. Do not agree with them but confront the untruth with the truth of Christ. This is the only way to defeat these forces. It is a spiritual warfare. It's not a battle of words but a warfare in the spirit world. So be sure to stand for righteousness and take no pleasure in the works of darkness.

Your soul will only project goodness and love and peace when it is secure in itself. It will project all else – it's fears and anxieties when it is not secure. It's the insecurities of the soul that give rise to defences to shield the soul from these fears. Only in Jesus can your soul be at peace. It is in Him that you will find peace of mind and heart. He is the One who is your Creator and only in your Creator will you find peace and rest. So when you feel anxious or threatened, submit to Christ. Do not get defensive for when you do, you regress and your fears are multiplied. Choose to love and Christ's love will fill you. That's why you choose to die to the flesh or give it control. These desires of the flesh will slowly loose their control over you as you acknowledge Jesus as Lord.

You don't have as much victory because you regress to fleshly modes of thinking. Recognise this. Acknowledge Jesus as Lord - acknowledge your dependence on Him. Your inner child will grow into security as you confess Him as the only Lord of your life. This is the only way to grow and move away from the path of destruction of your soul. The way of the flesh leads to increasing introspection. The way of the Spirit leads to life and creativity.

So submit yourself to the Spirit of Christ in you. He is the one who marks you as present. This life in the Spirit is only possible as you surrender all to Him. This is a process - so do not be alarmed. Confess all the weaknesses of the flesh - so the flesh has no need to defend itself. All selfishness and self-centredness must be crucified at the Cross. Now live in the new life in you. There is no liberty till the flesh is condemned to death. The flesh will always be your chief enemy. Now you can either give attention to the flesh through your senses or pay attention to the Spirit in you by faith. The way of the flesh is based on law. The way of the Spirit is based on love.

Only Jesus can save. It's only His presence in you and the active exercise of His presence in you will enable you to walk the walk of faith and exercise His gifts and fruits. Any other way is man's way. If you walk in defence then you will be walking in the flesh. You must come to the point where you give no place for the flesh to rejoice. You must come to the place where you can say I am nothing. This is the point at which God will take over and work in and through you. This is the only way. God in Christ demonstrated this as He walked on this earth. It's through prayer that you receive His fullness to walk in the light. All else is darkness. The Jews were a rejected race but God showed His love for them in establishing them as a nation and making them a special people. Now God used this nation as an example of His ways. He has now brought the Good News of His salvation to all peoples of all nations. Jesus has now become the Saviour of all who will choose Him. Whatever system you belong to will mould you into its shape. If you disagree with the system then the system will either tolerate you or reject you. Difference is not a comfortable place to be in. It's conformism that will result in institutionalism. It will take brave people to change the world. Jesus did not conform and so the Jews rejected him. He had to suffer this rejection.

Nuggets of Truth

- Materialistic spirit is in opposition to God's Spirit.
- Love at all times - direct all negatives to the cross.
- Making right choices.

- Living in the truth - actively believing and behaving in what you know is the truth.
- Differentiate a fantasy from imagination.
- Serving Christ in others.
- Releasing the real me through confession.
- Standard: Live each day in the fear of the Lord; that is, doing only that which is right and acceptable in His sight, dead to self- alive in Him.
- Be doers and less talkers.
- Rebuild, remake, and restore the parts of me into a whole - transformed by His Word of power.
- To live each day as if it is the last day.
- Each individual is so precious.
- Importance of communication - otherwise splitting will occur, projecting one's own badness onto others.
- Human suffering produces character.
- Invest in the inner life.
- Unconditional love.
- True freedom is within.
- Knowing that I am loved and valued.
- Faith is in a person- Jesus.
- Law of grace and love.
- Know who you are in Christ.
- Love acts - defence only reacts.
- No compromise - light and darkness are opposites.
- In the world, good and evil are compromised, in God they are separated.
- Walking in the light means total and complete surrender to Jesus.
- I am under the authority of Father God when I abide in Him.
- Concentrate on being.
- Confession of weaknesses, sins- clinging to the cross of Jesus.
- Man's need is for self-acceptance.
- Fact [truth] is that you are in Christ and can now operate from your new nature in Christ.

- Live for today.
- Kill the flesh by directing its desires to the cross - imagine the cross of Christ, all your sins laid on Him, and receive His love flowing to you.
- Free to think, feel and act as you would.
- It is not what you do or do not do that matters - it is the attitude of your heart.
- With the heart man intuits - with the head he decides.
- The false is an illusion; the real is in Christ.
- The false self cannot receive God's love.
- Identification and identity in Christ.
- Illusions, fantasies, are an escape from reality.
- Prayer is the answer to all situations in life - like breath.
- My pilgrimage through this earthly life is to die to self and be filled with Him- to be like Jesus.
- Prayer prepares the heart for receiving, living and being.
- Pray in tongues at all times to remain under His influence and all thoughts to be subjected to Him- less chance of operating in the flesh.
- Tap into the positive power of God- faith imagination.
- Pray and stay in faith- walking in hope, love and forgiveness.
- Seeing in the spiritual and speaking forth the word of faith.
- Looking for God's rhema Word- said Word and saying Word.
- All of us are victims of our past- real or imagined.
- Paralysed feelings lead to concrete thinking.
- When you ask, believe that you have received.
- Persist and persevere.
- Who I am determines how I behave.

Christ our reference point

What a marvellous salvation. Man can philosophise and it is all good but is not sufficient to save his soul. There is only one way. God has provided the way-Jesus Christ. All who know Him love Him.

Just as Jesus came to redeem all things to Him, so also you are to bring light in the midst of darkness. This is only possible through death. The light in you needs to shine. Don't be put off by the presentations of man. He is fallen. He is deceived. Satan is a master deceiver and all that follow him are deceived. You can believe in anything and to you it is right. This is deception. That's why Christ had to come. Christ is the only one who has overcome the evil one. No one else can or has. Everyone else is a form of the light. Satan, the god of this world, specialises in peripherals - what you eat, what you wear, holy days, fasting, penance, and suffering. God came to liberate man from these burdens, laws, traditions and fleshly works of man to attain salvation.

Life is to be lived. In Christ I will be directed by His Holy Spirit in me. When I let go of all things then I am free to be. There are things I hold on to. These thoughts, attitudes and desires have kept me locked in. Now in the Spirit I am free to be. The social mirror- the need to conform and seen to be acceptable, needs to be changed. I need to be motivated from within and not from without. As long as I live to please someone else I fail to grow- I become the captive of the one I am enslaved to - whether it be parents, partner, pastor, parlour or profession. The only way I can live is to be free to be a person who operates under His authority to be a channel of His love. There will be many pressures but the principles and life of my Saviour will always guide me. He is the point of reference. When there isn't a reference point then one will be swayed by everything that comes along. Television is a source of influence that influences our thoughts, feelings and behaviour. A person that does not have a point of reference will be easily persuaded. It's good to have knowledge and information but if this is not tested against a grid ie. one's belief system then one is easily influenced.

The Bible, God's Word is your reference book in all areas of conduct in life. Without this you are left to make up your own mind. In a world where everyone is taken up with their own opinions, it's only faith in One who never changes- the eternal Word of God- a person who lives forever and a life that is based on His life- resurrection life, that can stand against the confusing voices and sounds of the world. Forces ethereal influence the world and therefore one needs to be sure where one's feet are to stand. Governments, systems, policies come and go. However ones life is not based on these. Ones life is grounded on something more then these.

Jesus - our standard

Do not compare yourself with others for in doing this you will not grow into the image of Christ but into the image of another - an illusion. Jesus must be your standard in all areas of conduct and behaviour. He is the one who will judge you on that day when He will reward all those who have kept to the way. It's the compromise of man that has made him accept the lesser standard. Do not give in to this. A man of God must be filled with the Spirit of God and be led by Him. Pleasing others only leads to all kinds of compromises. You have to be a standard because you represent Jesus on earth. He is your eyes and ears and hands and feet. Consecrate all your members to Him. For in this way they will be used to glorify God and not self. Deny and kill every desire of the flesh to put itself above others and in front of others. Beware especially of your tongue. Love others in a pure sincere love and do not lead anyone astray. Lead them to the pure love of Jesus. His love is the only way out of the mess. His love is the only love that will truly satisfy. No other love satisfies like His. Knowing Him then will give you a security and a purpose that will enable you to love like Him. Always measure yourself against yourself and not against another. It is in the measuring of oneself against another that leads to all kinds of envy and jealousy. You are not answerable for another's behaviour and lusts. You can warn others but in the end each is responsible for his/her own behaviour.
So train yourself in loving and being in Him. For it is in living in His presence continuously that brings joy and peace. Living under the constraints of man leads to inhibitions and worries that lead to all kinds of problems and conflicts.

On being

So beware of the yeast of the flesh that leads to the adulteration of the spirit. Seek to live in purity. All the thoughts and lusts of the flesh only cause you to walk in the flesh. Direct them to the Cross of Christ. You are only safe under the shadow of His Cross. Under this you are safe from all attacks of the flesh, world and devil. They cannot have any power over you for His blood covers you. Now lift up your eyes and head and see His love filling you to overflowing. This is the pure kind of love. Stop analysing and begin to live. To be is to feel and think in the now. This is to be filled in the Spirit. This is to be free. Analysis only separates you from being and causes you to observe and not be a part. Observation is for understanding. Being is for living. Too much observation takes away the joy in living.

Each life is called for a purpose. So do not compare yourself with others. Rather encourage each other to come to the full purpose of life that each has been called to. Encourage Christ in each one to come forth in His fullness. Do not encourage the evil in each other for this only gives the devil a foothold to do his works of destruction.

Seeing with the eyes of Jesus

Each life is precious and has the mark of the Creator in him or her. So encourage this life in others. When you are filled with the life of God in you, then you will see with the eyes of Jesus. You will see the potential in each individual. When you are filled with Him then there is less chance for your own negatives to influence others. All the goodness of the Godhead will flow through you and you will be a source of healing and life to others. So concentrate on living in His presence always. For in this way you will be a positive influence to others. All the forces of evil will be pushed back as you take your position in Christ. His blood will cleanse the place where you are and others will come under the influence of God rather than the influence of the flesh, world or devil.

Identifications

The tyranny of the soul is due to the bad images of the past. These images of the past are through wrong identifications. This is why it is so important to be with people who are godly and will be the source of good identifications. So many of My people are crippled by wrong or bad identifications. They therefore are unable to receive from Me for they liken Me to the poor models or identifications of their childhood. Till they can come to a revelation of My love that is unconditional and free they will continue to be under the bondage of their old identifications. The new needs to replace the old if change is to occur. In all spheres of life it's what you have experienced that will dictate how you behave. Change can only occur as one gives up these old models and receives the new. The new received in Christ will replace the old as the Holy Spirit changes the inner man from glory to glory into His image. This is the process of sanctification as you are transformed from the old ways of thinking and doing to the new.

New life in Jesus

God in His infinite wisdom sent forth His Son to be the Person who many could see, feel and touch and be transformed into His image. This transformation is a spiritual operation by His Spirit as one receives in his spirit the revelation of the Son of God. This revelation comes, as one is open to God and His love. Forsaking all else and looking to Jesus is the only way one will be transformed into His glory.

Repentance key to forgiveness

When you have received forgiveness then you know what true freedom is. God's love is closely connected to His forgiveness. It is because He is a God of love that He forgives. However, His forgiveness is only released through repentance. To every fruit there is a key, so also the key to forgiveness is repentance. A repentant heart knows how to live in the love of God. It's only sinners that know and receive the love of God. Self-righteousness blocks God's love from reaching the heart of man. It's when man sets himself up on the basis of his own righteousness that leads to an unreceptive heart. When one appreciates God's love and forgiveness then there will be no place for pride and a self-righteous spirit but only humility and a spirit of graciousness.

God's salvation

Those who have tested the Lord have come to know Him as the great I am. He is the only one who is able to save. All those who come to Him will be blessed- will be saved. So come to Him and let Him bless you with His salvation full and free. He is the one who blesses and saves. There is no one like Him. He is the ever loving, ever present, Almighty transcendent and all encouraging God. When you know Him, you know life. He is present around you and in you. He is the Mighty one of Israel. Israel stands for God's chosen people. God's chosen people are His creation that have been washed and cleansed in the blood. This is the only way to enter His kingdom. God has made the way - now walk in it. God has revealed in these last days - His Son. His Son is now present to save and to bless. He is present now and He will save. All you need to be is an instrument of His peace. He is able to save all those who come to Him - completely. He is able to save completely because He saves for eternity. Oh, how He loves His creation. He loves completely those who come to Him. So trust Him. He is the Alpha and Omega of your faith. There is nothing left to do than bask in His completed work. Now all you need to do is to submit, obey and trust Him all the way. This then will release in you a power that nothing can stop. This power is released as you focus on His presence in you. Images of power, love, peace, kindness, joy will flow out through you. You won't be imaging on the fallen images of the flesh but on God in you. His presence in you is the guarantee that you are safe and secure. You won't need to be searching anymore but to be. To be is to live in His presence completely. Old conflicts and temptations will come but as long as you stay focused on the object of your faith then you will overcome.

See how today as you step outside of yourself - the old self, and not hide in it's perceived safety, that all the old fears and anxieties will fall away or lose their power over you - mere illusions, a fiction of your fallen imagination and you come present to your true self - the self that has been redeemed in Christ.

Seeking Gods way

God's love and forgiveness brings a person to the place of power with God. It's only a man who has come to the end of self who can appreciate what it means to be wholly submitted to Him and His ways. All other ways are man made solutions to His ways. To know God's way, one must be in tune with His Spirit in you. He is the one who will teach you His ways. His teaching is personal. He will not only enable you to understand His ways but also to do them. This is only possible as you leave all and seek in earnest to listen to His voice in you. All the other voices stemming from self and other spirits will want to dictate to you but only when you are earnest in subjecting them to death and only to listen to Christ will you come into total deliverance. Don't try to change people - only love them in Christ knowing that Christ loves them. It's only His love in you that will convince them of Me and cause a thirst in them to seek for Me. This thirst can only be satisfied by My living water. All other water only satisfies temporarily. I am the only Way. Only when man comes to Me will he be satisfied.

Affirmation

Calling forth the good in others is a sure way of affirming them and bringing them to a place of acceptance. Visualising them the way Christ sees them - saved in Him - is the way to relate with others - in love. Never try and put them down or look for their weaknesses. Pray that you may see their positives and call their positives forth that they may be encouraged and uplifted. There is enough evil in this world and most people need to be affirmed and loved. Do not be deceived by the superficial front they project but see Christ in them. As you affirm them as persons, they will lower their masks and receive His goodness through you.

False self and feelings

All the negativity that is evoked in oneself emanates from the false self.
When the false self is threatened then the feelings associated will come forth. The spirit behind the feelings will begin to manifest itself. It was kept under control by the defences that keep all our negative and hostile feelings at bay. However, in crises, or under threat to our security or significance, these fears are brought out. Now direct them to the Cross. The other maybe perceived as the accuser but the feelings are yours and cannot be blamed on the other. The other was just one who threatened you and evoked those feelings. If the feelings were not there then they couldn't have been evoked.

Sin and repentance

There is too much emphasis on legitimising sin, by positively condoning it. This appears respectable, but the basic problem is not confronted. Change is seen as a way to accommodate to sinful behaviour. This approach may arise from the premise that man is basically good. However the Bible says that man is basically sinful. Education and sophistication of behaviour has just covered it up. It is this sophistication that prevents man from coming in touch with his basic selfishness and sinfulness, that is accepted as present day enlightenment - nudist camps, free sex, etc.
God's call for change is through repentance of attitudes and behaviours that are basically sinful, self-centred to Christ-contredanses and deliverance from the power of sin.

Sin of introspection

Neurotic defences always direct feelings onto others, or creates reasons rather than facing up to issues. Concentrating on the here and now-cuts away sin of introspection. Sin is a sickness that can only be overcome by resting in the finished work of Christ on the Cross and by abiding in Him.

Introspection - kill it. The only way to kill it is to be involved with others and make the most of it. Sin leads to introspection, which leads to fears and vain imaginations, which lead to sickness. When your will is free to choose you can do anything. All habits can be broken - decision, perseverance and faith in God. You can influence others by choosing to be Christ to them.

Sin and salvation

Sin brought a turning of self inwards and thus the darkness had to be coped in some way. For this, defensive walls were put up to shut off the light of God. Thus Man was confined to walk in blindness. Then God in His mercy shone His light and the defences broke down and the light shone in my darkness and I saw. God had entrance into my life and came and dwelt in me. I was born again-now able to discern good from evil. Yet I continued to hold on to the familiar. So God now is at work in me to transform me by delivering me from my old self into my new identity in Him. He does this by loving me till I give up my old selfish ways and choose to deny myself, take up my cross and follow Him. He is always there and is leading me through life despite myself. I enjoy His abundance when I submit all to Him.

Saintliness and sinfulness

There is a fine line between saintliness and sinfulness. This is why it is so confusing to one who chooses to walk the broad way of life. The narrow way keeps me walking in the way of holiness, discipline and constant vigilance to the evil within and without that seek to enter and infiltrate the holy of holies. God - the Holy Spirit resides in the holy place in you. Yet your soul images evil, lust and pride and there seeks to attack the Holy Spirit - who dwells in your spirit. This is the way power is sapped. Without the life giving initialising power of the Holy

Spirit - your spirit is like a dry desert, parched and lifeless. Your soul - thoughts, feelings and will needs to come under the induement of the Holy Spirit. This is only possible as you give your senses (flesh) and your soul to Him - to His control. He will wash and cleanse your soul and your flesh or body so that no evil can touch you. A cleansed vessel is like pure light that outshines the darkness. The darkness of the soul is what keeps the light of the spirit from being seen and heard.

Sinful flesh

All my reactions of the flesh humble me to see who I really am in the flesh - sinful through and through. So now I turn all these unrighteous and selfish desires to Him and rest in His pure light. I will not be condemned for I am free in Him. I will direct all those condemning voices, thoughts and feelings to Him for He is the Keeper of my soul. I will rejoice in Him. He is able to keep that which I have committed to Him. Now I will live freely knowing that each moment He gives me to enjoy life to the full knowing that His will is the best for me. So whatever may come my way, I shall rejoice in His salvation. I shall choose to walk the way of love and not give in to my fears or to the pressure of others who want to live compromised lives. I will look to Him. My eyes will be fixed on Him. I will not look to the outward form but the inward life that is eternal.

Sin controls you

Be vulnerable and get rid of the evil within you. This is the only way. An unconfessed sin will continue to control you. People become sick because of this. It is only Jesus who can liberate and set free. The indwelling Jesus by the Holy Spirit dispels all darkness and sin. So confess and do not hold back. As long as you are confessing your own sin no one can condemn you. Don't judge others but by example confess your sin. In the Spirit you can accomplish a lot. Remember God is in control and what you bind on earth is bound in heaven. So commit all to God and pray. Pray in tongues - visualise the situation and see the mountains being moved. God is merciful.

He will remove the barriers. All He needs is your complete surrender. It always happens. When you hold on to something then you bind Gods hands in the situation. Only complete surrender works. It is the spirit that enables. People pick up the spirit. A spirit of control will not work for you but against you. Let go and let God. This is what the disciples had to learn. The Holy Spirit came and anointed them with power. He responded to their faith with power from on high. Faith is obedience. There is no faith without obedience. Faith encourages obedience. Faith enables obedience. You are in control of your will to choose. If you do not have control over your thoughts then it is because you have surrendered it to another. Only one you can surrender to is to God. Anyone you give control to will control you. You then experience the feelings of being manipulated and controlled. These feelings come because of a loss of control or giving up control to the forces around you. Step back - commit to God and see how you can exercise control over the situation. Cooperation is good but not at the expense of your own self-respect and dignity. You need to stand against the forces that will try and overpower you to control you. No - you must stand. Whether in small things or large - commit to God in prayer - every situation, feeling, thought and person that seeks to control you otherwise you come under the control of the person, thought or feeling. In the Holy Spirit you can do this. This way you develop the fruit of self-control or delayed gratification.

Jesus waited - for He knew God was in control. He kept the faith, ran the race and defeated Satan. Satan was tricked into believing that he had the ultimate weapon but he fell into his own trap and lost the control of the fear of death. Jesus overcame death through His resurrection - so I can now live not in the fear of death but in the experience of resurrection life.

Crucify the flesh

No one can correct you as long as you live a crucified life. What is negative is of the flesh and needs to die. You can't do anything about it but to crucify it. So if you deny yourself and crucify your flesh then there is no need to talk about it. It is when you fail to walk in the fullness of the Spirit that these negatives will well up in you.

Where is the source for all the pride, jealousy, envy, murder and hatred? It is in the flesh life. So any stirring's of this kind need to be crucified. There is no other way. Commit all to God and live in righteousness. Do not allow those feelings to get on top of you for they are not of God - they are of the flesh fuelled by hell itself. So don't try and compare yourself with others. For this will only produce competition and all other kinds of evil. Be humble and know your own frail and sinful state. Live for what you know is right whatever the odds for God is with you and that is what matters. Giving in to evil ways only opens up the door for Satan to come in and destroy. So be on guard. Plead the blood of Jesus in situations where evil seems to have the upper hand - this is your only protection as Satan cannot stand the mention of His Blood. Purify yourself. Don't be pulled by the negative forces of the past for you have been set free from its influence. Your yesterdays are blotted out for like the dead it is forgiven and forgotten so that you can be freed from its influence and are able to live in the fullness of the Spirit today.

Keep to the right

Know what is right and stick to it. The opposition may be fierce but a man who knows God will not compromise.

Whatever the darkness that comes against you, keep this in mind and never give in to a negative spirit. Feelings come and go. Negative feelings abound where there is no love. Satan will attack because he thrives in a negative atmosphere. Your responsibility is to plead the blood of Christ and direct all those forces to the Cross of Jesus. Do not receive them or analyse them.

Voices of the past

There is enough to face up to today and you will need all the strength you can get to live today.

So be free today from those negative voices of your past. Direct them to the Cross. These voices have no more power over you. Do not listen to them for they waste your time. Know that I am the One who keeps you. So be strong and very courageous and release all the power of heaven today by walking by faith in the finished work of Christ on the Cross. Never look back- look up and ahead and keep your mind and heart fixed on the One who lives to make intercession for you. Let Him free you for He is at work in you to release you into His abundance, which you can then share with others.

Liberty in Jesus

So live today and rejoice in His love and liberty for Christ lives in you.
The knowledge of God in you will sustain you through all the storms of life. Most of the storms in life are caused through relationships. This is why Jesus came and offered His life up so that He could show us the way of true relationship. A relationship that gave up all, that I may receive love and fellowship from God the Father. A relationship that sacrificed that I may be free from the power of sin. So as you tap into God's love -unconditional love, then you will not only feel free but also be free to love your fellow men.
He will protect you from the darts of the evil one. It is important to discern the difference between the sins of the flesh and the influence of spirits. In all negative situations you not only open yourself up or are vulnerable to your own negativity but to that of the other and the influence of evil spirits. However a strong sense of your position in Christ will enable you to withstand these pressures from others and from the evil one. It's the knowledge of His sacrifice on the Cross that will enable you to stand free for He will absorb all the negativity in the situation. So learn to direct all that to the Cross so that you may be free.

Suffering

Just as Jesus came to suffer and to die so also you have been

called to suffer at the hands of men for righteousness sake. You don't suffer for doing evil things but for righteousness. Hold to that which is right and your actions will be righteous. Hold to that which is right, good and true and you will experience His love and peace and joy.
Once you have tasted His love, joy and peace, then you will sacrifice all to experience His love, joy and peace at all times. So do not be surprised if you experience troubles in this life. Always know that when you choose to do right, you will become stronger in Him and prevail despite all odds.
So do not avoid conflict or trouble but fix your mind and heart in Him and be strong. He will lead you through paths that lead to abundant life for His ways always satisfy. So cling to Him and His ways. Look to Him for strength, wisdom and power. Do not be overwhelmed by the feelings, words and actions of others but know that He who holds you is the One who will see you through to the end.
Therefore, be glad and rejoice at all times and be thankful. He is the One who has led you and been with you through thick and thin and will see you through to the last day. So do not be fearful or anxious of what lies before you. Live each day to the full. When the fires blow hot remember that He was with Daniel and his friends and they were not singed.
It is in the identification with the sufferings of others that you become their source of deliverance. A person who is prepared to suffer with others will know what it means to suffer like Christ did. Jesus did not suffer for His own sins but for the sins of others. In such suffering you complete the sufferings of Christ in your body. This is to be identified with His death.
Suffering for righteousness sake. So do not judge others for in judging them you put yourself apart from them and will not be able to serve them.
There is so much suffering in this world. Most of it is in silence. For this world and all in it is doomed to eternal damnation. Therefore nothing is without pain. This is the result of the fall. God controls the whole world. The devil is a defeated foe and he can only have mastery over your life when you take your eyes off Him. So do not be distracted. At every attack or subtle longing of the flesh turn to Him and see Him

attack your enemies and defeat them. As you continue to live in this way, you will find that the new life is truly abundant.

Contentment

Praise Him at all times and in all places and see the victory that will follow you wherever you go. Faith in God leads to power in His sovereignty over all things. Praise fuels power that releases the resources of heaven. God has given you the keys that you need to use to release His resources. Now, as you praise Him, He will guide you in mysterious ways. All things will be in your favour. So walk and talk as His representative on earth and see how favour will flow toward you. Do not judge as man judges- rather leave all to God and let Him be your judge. Only strive to do your best and expect the best. He has called you to abundant life. The key to abundant life is contentment. This is what releases the abundant life in you. When you are content in all situations knowing that God is with you then you know the secret of abundant life. This life is for living. Now release yourself from all your ways and look to God to guide you and lead you. Have high goals in all areas of your life. Do not be satisfied with the basics. See how all things will be released to you as you walk in His ways. Much is given to you that you may give much. Abundant living is not to keep to yourself but to share. So enlarge your heart. See how I shall open the heavens and bless you. A man who is committed to Him and to His purposes need fear nothing for He is with him. He will release all things to him at the opportune time.
Not all will be revealed so that you will learn to walk by faith and not in the confidence of your flesh. Faith in Jesus is the only requirement. All things are possible to them that have faith. For He is God of all things and He runs all things in heaven and on earth. So you as His child can tap into His resources in heaven. Only those who belong to Him and trust in Him can do this. So be an example and see how you can lead others also into this truth.
The Lord is good and His mercies endure forever. The devil will try to focus your attention on one specific sin and make you

oblivious to others. In this way he can condemn you for this one sin and keep you in bondage. He is a master trickster and therefore resist him. Do not allow time or circumstances to dull you into a false sense of security. Be vigilant at all times and be in the Spirit. For you cannot operate in the Spirit and walk in the flesh. Pray always in the Spirit. For in this way you will stay pure in heart and mind. Do not come into condemnation. Remember His blood flows continuously and you experience its effects as you receive by faith the cleansing. Only His blood can cleanse and free. As you experience this cleansing you will want to share it with others. Do not fear man but be what you are and others will honour you.

Remember He is Creator of all things and He died for all mankind, that all may come into the knowledge of His salvation. So be bold and do not be threatened but be firm. Your real identity is in Him and you live out of your false self when you do not live from His life in you.

Whatever you fix your gaze on will influence you. If it's evil or the lusts of the flesh, then these lusts will possess you. Many come under demonic influence in this way. They give in to the lusts of their flesh and so come under their influence. This then takes over their life and possesses them. You be careful therefore that Jesus is Lord of your life at all times so that these other influences cannot control you.

Jesus is Lord

You can be sensitive to others feelings or the spirit underlying those feelings. Be careful to always acknowledge the Lordship of Jesus in your life so that you do not see in others what is really possessing or influencing you. If Jesus is not Lord then some other spirit is in control. This is what leads to conflicts. Where Jesus is Lord then no other spirit can influence the group or individual. This is why it is so important not to allow yourself to come under the influence of another for when you do so out of fear of man then you put yourself in bondage. This is not submission but bondage. True submission can only occur when one is submitted to someone higher. One who is submitted to God the Father will be able to submit himself to others. For then he does not submit himself to bondage for he is under the influence of One greater than the one he is submitting to.

Truth is in a person

Truth is not in words but in a Person. When you know the person you know His thoughts and intentions. Truth in the person is different from truth that is in the physical realm. These truths are discovered. Truth that is not physical is intuited. Such truth cannot be discovered through the laws of science. What is revealed to you through the Spirit covers physical laws. The Spirit is above physical and emotional spheres. Therefore when you are in communication with the Spirit, you will have access to all truth. God will reveal to you what you will need to know. This is why Jesus could deliver, heal and alter the physical forces - change water into wine. He operated in the Spirit.
If you operate only in the physical realm, then you will be limited to this. But if you operate from the Spirit then you will be operating from above and will have insight into all things. This is why it's important to move in the Spirit. Knowledge that is limited to the physical realm only reveals half the truth. In the world there is darkness. In every soul there is darkness. If it was not for the darkness then no evil could abide. The very fact that evil is seen and heard means that darkness is prevalent in this world. As long as the god of this world (Satan) has power on this earth, there will be darkness and every kind of evil. This will be seen and heard in different ways. However the light always overcomes darkness. Darkness can never overcome light. Therefore you can have confidence that just as light overcomes darkness, so the light in you will overcome the darkness in others and around you as you walk in His light. It's only His light that can overcome the darkness in you. Beware of pride and every other lust of the flesh. These all encourage a walk in the darkness and not in the light. So be holy, as He is holy. For it is the holiness of God that will ultimately prevail over darkness. No knowledge of man is adequate.

Forces of good and evil

What you choose to do releases spiritual forces. The forces of evil or good. The flesh or the devil will work against the Holy Spirit. Therefore when you are filled with the Holy Spirit you work against the flesh and the devil. This is the way it is. It's your will that needs to be surrendered. When you do this the Holy Spirit gets to work to influence your mind in His ways changing your thoughts and feelings resulting in changed perceptions. He will release His mind to you. You will see things differently and therefore be able to respond differently.

This is what the Spirit has been sent to do. With the Holy Spirit are a whole host of angels and spiritual beings that help the saints to live a life wholly unto him. This world and its pressures keeps you caged, imprisoned to this world system dominated by the evil ruler of this age, Satan. So don't be surprised that the people of this world cannot see for they are blinded by the flesh and the devil to see and do things that are self-centred and not God centred. When you invite the Holy Spirit to rule in you then you crucify the flesh and rule in the Spirit.

So come my child and live like a king - He is in you. He will lead you and guide you. He will speak through you. So be confident. Just learn to flow with him. No hurdles will be too high for you. Don't be distracted by the pressures and hurdles of this world. You can overcome because the overcomer is in you. Only be sure to be led by the Holy Spirit at all times.

Just speak and do as He leads and you will be on the right track. This calls for faith, for being. To live with integrity is to live in unity in mind and spirit and the body will follow. All systems will flow smoothly as the Holy Spirit comes in and fills you to overflowing. He will soothe your mind and body. He will control every system in and out because He is free to control all things through you.

This is the inheritance of the children of God. This is why you need to give all control to Him. The flesh seeks to glorify itself. It speaks for God but the intention of the flesh is to glorify itself. It's only a crucified man who knows what it means to give up all things to glorify God. This is the stumbling block - the flesh. Come by faith in the Holy Spirit to overcome your fleshly longings. It is possible but only in the Spirit.

The power of God is available to all that call to Him. God is the Creator of all Creation. He is the only Creator. We are all created by Him. We therefore belong to Him and are loved by Him. There is no distinction. We all belong to one family. However sin entered this world and brought a division between good and evil. Before this all was good. Evil entered the heart of man. Now man was separated from His Creator. The creative process continues but evil resides with good in man. Man now had become independent of his Creator and this independence gives him a choice. What good he chooses is of his Godly inheritance and what evil he chooses is of his evil nature. Now man has a choice either to serve God or mammon. This is why one sees so much good in an evil world. This good needs to be encouraged. All good work is to produce good or for the good of man and to fight evil. This fight against evil can be done in one's own strength or in the strength of God. Man has devised ways to fight evil. Where there is good, evil is close by to attack all the good that man does. This pollution therefore continues to infiltrate and pollute the life of man and society as a whole.

In Christ a man is delivered from the power of sin and the evil one. Evil has been overcome through the death of Christ on the Cross. As a Christian focuses his eyes on the Cross then all evil within him is cancelled as His blood cleanses and delivers. All one needs to do is to stay fixed in this faith position to prevail. Through the resurrection of Christ man has been delivered from his evil ways and brought into the light of Christ.

This is why Christians have to be a light to the world that is still in darkness, because of the evil in them, that overpowers them. They have to fight this evil in their own strength for they do not know Christ. Christ is available to all that will call upon Him. In Him there is no Jew or Greek, slave or free. In Him all are one. So you have the light in you. Where He is there is no darkness. Let the consciousness of darkness in you cause you to repent and renounce the evil within you that you may be cleansed and delivered. See this darkness as separate from the real you in Me that is in Christ. Do not give it attention but rather overcome it by identifying with Christ. It's as you do this that you will prevail and overcome.

Selfishness

The source of all the pain, mistrust and conflict in this world is selfishness. There is no end to this as long as we live in "this" fallen world. It is only in seeking after God that a breakthrough can occur. I live to serve, O Lord this is the only way.
Because of pain and trauma and loss, people tend to look for saviours who will deliver them from their pain and distress. They look to others to meet this need. They will never find it. It is only in looking to God that you will find fulfilment. For God who created you can meet every need of yours - spiritual, emotional and physical. Just think, He is the creator of the whole world and all that is in it. Put your trust in Him. This is the only way to be fulfilled. It is only when this need of yours to be loved can be fulfilled that you will be able to live like a minister unto the Lord. You will only be fulfilled as you choose to die to the flesh - selfish, self-centred and sinful ways to Christ-centred, Holy Spirit empowered ways that serve to minister.
God's love surrounds you and encapsulates you from the negative influences of this world. His love is what shields you and keeps your hope alive knowing that your eternity is assured and that in Him all things are possible. God is able to make something out of nothing. So as you put your faith and trust in Him, you become a person who has potential - potential to make things happen, to bless, to contribute to others lives so that this negative world will be blessed. You will be so filled with Him, that you cannot but love. All hatred, unbelief and faithlessness will be banished. All you want to do is love and bless because God is a positive God. He came to give life. Death is the consequence of sin. Man can choose life or death. You have chosen life. So do not allow the negative influence of this world to influence you. You have nothing to

do with it. Get yourself always into a positive state. Once your mind is in a positive state then your responses will be positive. If the negative situation or person is able to get you into a negative state then your responses will be accordingly. So keep yourself in a positive state of mind always. When you find yourself drifting into a negative state keep pressing the positive buttons till you are able to enter a positive, overcoming state. Your state will determine your responses. Don't respond when you get into a negative state. This is the way to be an overcomer.

All is selfishness, all is death. There is no purpose beside the knowledge of God. All is doomed to death and decay. How man prides over his achievements as if they were eternal. Only God is eternal. Therefore, do not deceive yourself. You are nothing as a man. But the Holy Spirit lives in you. Look to Him to fill you with the eternal things of the Kingdom of God that last forever. This is where your heart should be - fixed on Him.

There is no other place for peace and joy but in the bosom of Christ. He is the one who gave all, now, only by giving all to Him is there true release. All the pressures of the world, the flesh and the devil, will not be able to overturn you because your life is built on the Rock that never moves.

So come to the fountain that never stops and be immersed in it. Let Him fill your soul and be refreshed. Be bold and be earnest in all your desires according to the Holy Spirit. All other desires will fade away as you keep yourself locked into the Christ who lives in you. Abide in Me, says the Lord, then you will be free from all your oppressors. They will flee like the wind because the Victor lives in you to prevail and to overcome all your enemies. Walk in love and the peace of God that passes all understanding, will keep your heart and mind in Christ Jesus.

Personal relationship with God

God is above all our puny systems and beliefs. This is why Jesus Christ came to destroy the rules and traditions of man and to bring him to a personal knowledge of Himself. This is above all system. It is a life lived in personal relationship with

One who is God. This is the difference between religion and Christianity.

One must respect others for what they believe. To them this is important. Their fragile sense of self depends on this. It's cruel to reject or challenge another's belief, for in so doing, one is challenging the very core of his being. However there is no law against loving another. Accepting the person but trying to understand his beliefs. He is also a product of his environment. Through Christ's life in you, you can begin to challenge his belief and win him over to Christ.

Jesus came to save and deliver - not to condemn. However anyone who does not believe is already condemned.

His life - not beliefs

We are called to be Christ's love offerings - messengers spreading His love - not our system of beliefs. Finally it's not doctrine but the person Jesus Christ that saves. Therefore my chief responsibility is to witness to His life. His life is above systems. His life is in me and He wants me to communicate His life to others.

I do this by relating with Him. It's not my beliefs. My beliefs will always be challenged. However, His life in me will speak louder than my words. It's my security in Him that counts. So it is not in my dress, where I live, or what club I belong to - but Jesus in me - that is the source of life. If others can come and taste Jesus in me, then they will know.

Therefore free yourself from the systems and structures and step out of them. That's your prison. Now you have been given new life - so step out and begin to live. Like a butterfly that breaks out of its cocoon - break forth into liberty. Do not fear but trust in the Lord. Live to influence. It's a man who fears that needs a cage. One who knows the Redeemer walks, talks and lives as one free to be a person who lives in a dimension above the human systems. Many are trapped in this. So free yourself now from these and see how you can be different - see, feel and hear from a higher plane where Jesus sits in heavenly places and be His witness of His love and power here on earth.

God is moving in you to break you, to soften your heart so that He can pour His love into you and you can soak in it. A hard heart cannot receive for it will be like water off a duck's back. Only a broken spirit can God heal. A hardened heart is like stone that will resist any change. When the stone was rolled away - Jesus came forth. So also the stony heart needs to break, so Jesus can come forth.

Cross and salvation

The Holy Spirit within you is at work. It's only your will that needs to cherish the Cross. The Cross will work in you to make you receptive to His words, feelings and thoughts. The Holy Spirit in you is the Teacher, Guide and Friend. The Holy Spirit in you will cause you to repent and turn away. All the thoughts that assail you should make you cling to the Cross. The Cross will cancel the power of those thoughts. Christ chose the way of the Cross because he knew there was no other way to resurrection life. He had to go through it. So you also need to reckon yourself dead so that you too can come into the anointing. There will be various pressures on you but remember always that God is in you to make you a person after His desires and plan. He will anoint you when He sees you yearning for Him and His love. When you move in His love then there is nothing else to compare. His love is free and is for all.
Repentance is the key to death to the flesh life. Without the Cross there is no resurrection. Without death to the flesh there is no resurrection life. So come to Him - visualise Him - who died for you that you might receive new life. This is why the Cross is the only way. This is not the way of the world. So every thought, feeling, intention, needs to be brought down- deadened- killed off that stands in the way of the Spirit in your life. The Holy Spirit in you operates in love, peace and joy- not in envy, jealousy, lust, hatred or pride. So you know what spirit is possessing you at any one time. You have the discerning of spirits to know. So don't be alarmed by these attacks of the devil. Every attack is an indication of an area of your life that needs to die. So listen to those thoughts and

deaden them through repentance, application of the Cross and blood. This is the most powerful way of deliverance. This is Christ's way of healing for the soul. There is no other way. Everything else is a softened or human means to salvation.
Christ died once for all. Now either I accept this message or go the broad way that leads to death.

Principles of the Kingdom

Christ's way leads to life. See how you are attracted to His message. You know this is the way for you .Now walk in it. Don't get caught up in the deceptiveness of the flesh but resign yourself to this one thing - Christ's way is the best way- way of love- of laying down one's life- no self-seeking but only seeking to bless- to give out of His riches in glory- not in my strength, but His. When I give myself to Him, then He will give Himself to me. Now I am free for I live for Him and I receive all His resources to do His will. Hallelujah, what a Saviour.
God's man is always eager to know His will. Therefore he will be content to submit his will to God's will. This is a man of faith. He moves at God's bidding. He is prepared to wait for God's time. For he knows that God is in control and God always shows up at the right time. God's time is not according to man's time. His purposes are higher than mans. However God chooses to work according to His principles of love and peace. God works through men who are submitted to Him and His kingdom principles.
Without these there is only hot air. It appears good and tangible but does not last. It promises but never delivers. His promises are true, built on His Word. His Word is eternal and never changes. Man may twist it, but His Word never changes. His principles never change because they are backed up by His power. Those that apply His principles will be assured of His power and presence.
Therefore live your life according to His Kingdom principles. These are like precious stones that will influence your thoughts and feelings and will to do. His Spirit within you works according to these principles. His Spirit cannot work in any other way. God never transgresses His Word. His life and

Word go together. His Word is the source of power for life. His life is not separated from His Word. The Word and life go together - that's why John said in the beginning was the Word (personal pronoun) and the Word became flesh or life. So also it's as you receive His Word to you today - it becomes His life. It's like bread - you eat it and it produces life - it satisfies your hunger and the elements in it causes you to grow. Without food you will be stunted.

His Word is like manna from heaven. It causes you to hunger for it and it satisfies your soul. Your soul becomes rich with spiritual manna. This then nourishes your soul. Your soul is enlarged. You begin to see things the way God sees and so your vision is enlarged. You don't get bogged down in introspective thoughts but your sights are lifted to heaven above. So you grow in stature as you feed on His Word.

Word of God

This is God's plan for you. To be completely submitted to His ways. It's His life in you that will cause others to want to know Him. It's not just words but works. Jesus preached the Word and souls were delivered from captivity. So a man's words can bless or bind. If your words flow from the life of the Holy Spirit within you then you sow seeds of life. This seed is then watered by the Holy Spirit as you pray. So pray much for those that you have close contact with. Pray that they too may come into the experience of knowing Him. You will sow out of what you have. Anything else is just words-good to the ears but does not have life.

Jesus spoke what He heard His Father tell Him - it was a personal Word - not just a philosophy - some creation of man's fallen state. Therefore His Words had power to give life - because it was from the Father, the Creator of all things. The Creator produces life, because His Word creates. It does not destroy. So you know what spirit is behind the words - if it creates, it is God's word. If it destroys, it is from another source. So, be separate-be God's man - be His disciple.

Adam's sin - Jesus death

One mans sin brought forth death – another's death brought life. Jesus Christ paid the price. This was Gods solution to the sin of man. When Adam the father of man sinned, all sinned through this one act. It is not Eve's sin but Adam's sin that had its effect on God. God had created Adam in His own image. Eve was created out of Adam to be his helpmate. God took responsibility for this and Jesus came to pay the price. The price was paid on Calvary. Jesus had to identify with Adam before His sacrifice was acceptable to God. God accepted the sacrifice. Now all those who put their faith in Christ-in His finished work - have life, eternal life. Death came through Adam - life through Christ. Now I can operate as Christ for His Spirit lives in me. However I am still in the flesh. My flesh continues to rule my body. My spirit is ruled by God in me. He has breathed His Spirit into me and therefore I am born again. Just as God breathed His breath into Adam, He has breathed His breath into me.

Now as I believe, put my faith in His revealed Word, I become like Him. I no longer follow the old script of the flesh but I am continuously renewed in my mind according to the mind of God. I am transformed into His image - His image is inside me and as I do, then I reflect His

image. When I walk in the Spirit, I reflect His image - His love, peace and joy. God has redeemed me. It is finished. The work has been done. Now I live by faith in His finished work.

Man is a spirit being

God is spirit. Man is spirit - created in the image of God. Man can therefore commune with God. He is orphaned without fellowship with God. His spirit however has been cut off from God through the fall. However he still has the capacity to know that there is something missing in his life. This search for the missing part of him is what leads him to seek for what is beyond this physical world. He therefore searches to find meaning in life. In his search he will be faced with various ways that promise him fulfilment. He tries these ways. Some give him an illusion of satisfaction. Some ways indoctrinate him to certain rules and regulations. He lives in the illusion of a spiritual experience but never is satisfied but accepts this as something better than nothing. Finally some come into a personal experience of salvation in Christ. There then begins a battle for the soul - the mind, will and emotions. Self and the world come in conflict with the Holy Spirit. He needs to decide who will control his life. Many fall on the wayside through this struggle. Some enter into the holy of holies. Others continue to struggle. Others are led astray.

A Spirit filled man decides to follow Christ - the Holy Spirit in him. He now no longer is led by his senses but by the Spirit. This is an ongoing struggle. If he listens to his senses then he is walking according to the flesh. The only way he can overcome the flesh is to walk in the spirit. This is where the warfare is. The battle for the mind. Walking according to the spirit allows the mind to know what the spirit says. The mind can then decide and take action. However the world, flesh and the devil conspire to war against the spirit of man. This is the place to take up the Cross. The Cross taken up everyday leads to death to self. Self is always in opposition to the spirit. This is why only complete consecration to God is able to keep you in His ways. There is no other way. God is able to completely save you when you give yourself completely to Him. This means complete submission and surrender to Him. This means being a slave to the Holy Spirit. It's only this attitude that will bring you into complete deliverance. Nothing else matters. All these things will loose their attraction. It's not a giving up of these things but a laying down of these things. Giving up is a work of the flesh. You are called to be in this world but you are not of it. All God has given you is to be received as a blessing from Him. However you live as one who owns nothing. All you look forward to is to be with the Father. When you release all then you are ready to leave. Then God can use you. For this world does not hold any more attraction for you. All you want to do is to glorify Him.

Taking up one's cross

This is death to self. This is total commitment. This is to take up one's cross. Don't worry what your brother does. Take it as a personal call from God for you. Let God use you. Let God deal with your brother. Now live each day listening to His spirit in you and live. Let joy and love flow freely. This is your inheritance in Christ- so rejoice and be glad. This is true freedom. Whatever you want to hold on to or want to control is an idol and needs to be destroyed. When you possess nothing then you have nothing to loose even your own life. So release all to Him and live as a saint.

Power of the tongue

The tongue that speaks on behalf of God is one that will bless and not divide. Your tongue is of God so be careful what you say. It will cause what you speak. Before you speak bring all to the Cross. The Cross will cancel out all negative influences. The Cross is your only way out of this world and its influences. The Cross of Jesus stands as evidence to the powers of this dark world that Jesus is Lord. He has subdued the forces of evil that conspire to destroy. There are examples since the beginning of time of the forces of evil. When evil words are spoken they go out into the atmosphere and reap a harvest of destruction. But before you speak you would have those thoughts. So beware of your thoughts. Words are just the body for the thoughts. Where do these thoughts come from? Subject them to the Cross.

The power of the Cross

The Cross will cancel out all thoughts from sources other then from God. The Cross before me means that the way forward in the will of God cannot be in any other way. The world behind me. The world will only be behind you when the Cross is before you. So look up and do not give in to the lusts of the flesh or the influences in the world. Resist them. Confront them by placing the Cross between you and them and see how they will flee. Only God's thoughts can face the Cross. All other thoughts will just melt away. In this way you will experience the power of the Cross. This is the only way to victory. No other way for a Christian. The Cross is the only way. That's why Jesus said I am the Way. All other ways have similarities but the Cross is the only way to eternal life. It's like other ways have the body but not the soul. People worship the body - like worshipping the building but not the builder. Other religions also purport to show the way but only Christ's sacrifice on the Cross is sufficient. The message of the Cross has been so watered down that there is no power left but those who come to the Cross will continue to be saved.

Trinity working together

God's love can be experienced. It is real. His love can set the captive free. So true freedom is internal. It is to be free from the negative influences of the past, the untruthful negative influences of the past. It is this freedom that will release individuals to operate freely in the present. God is in the healing business. You need power from on high to heal, to deliver in His Name. So come to Him with open hands to receive from Him freely. His blood cleanses- all can be cleansed, healed and delivered through His blood. The only answer to the sin problem is His blood. There is no other way. The Holy Spirit is the person who applies His blood. The 3 must go together. His Word reveals the truth, the Holy Spirit applies the truth and the blood delivers the captive - spirit, soul and body. Emphasis on one is only a partial application of the truth. The 3, Father provides the word, Jesus provides His blood and the Holy Spirit applies it. All 3 are working together. That's why we pray in the Name of the Father, Son and Holy Spirit. Faith is the key. Faith grasps this truth and runs with it. It's as you run with it that the deliverance will flow. The lepers went on their way believing and got healed on the way. I receive this truth and believe it and now I will experience it.

Fact 1 You are loved
Fact 2 You are cleansed in His blood

Fact 3 You are now free
Fact 4 You are a minister of His deliverance
Fact 5 Go in His power and live in His operating power.

Faith in the glorified life of Christ

Which side of the resurrection do you live in? I live in the glory of Christ for Christ was glorified and sits at the right hand of his Father - our Father in heaven. Those who glory in the Cross and not the resurrection, live a life of poverty. Christ died - now I identify with his death to sin - now I glory in his resurrection and I identify in His resurrection power. So by faith I can do all things in the risen Christ. Because he is risen, I am able to do all things. I am able to move mountains by faith. At the word of His command, I will move. I will live to praise His works. He is able to sow thoughts into me that will release resurrection power to heal, save, restore and reveal His love. He is abundantly able to do more than I can think or see - for He is able and therefore I am able. I will look to Him and all the mountains will be brought to a plane for me to walk through. This is the faith venture - in all areas, physical, emotional, and spiritual. God and I can break through and win.

Remedy

Connecting with God's power source is the way to release the creative power of God in you. You find that as you step out in faith in all areas of your life that fresh revelation and power are released. Don't fear only trust. Have goals but always be dependent on God's power to see you through. Be spontaneous. God will blot out from your memory system all the old fears and torments that plagued you for years by the deceitfulness of sin. Act in the present. It is the action in the present that will open doors in the future. Don't be taken up with having to put right the past - commit it to Jesus. He will take care of it. Now is the day to live to the full. Tomorrow is another day - today is the day to live by faith knowing that each day is given to you by God's grace to fulfil His

commission to do His will. You are God's representative - so do not be caught up with the affairs and conflicts of this world system. You are to be light. Uphold that which is good. Be solutions focused. Don't get caught up with theories and positions that uphold the system - you will get paralysed. Rather move out in faith to be creative for it is in being creative that you will receive the new idea to unblock all problems. The problems of life are created through stuckness and failure to grow - to stagnate and become stuck in a rut. This stuckness leads to a blinkered vision. It keeps to the straight and narrow. This is what a pessimist is like. His language behaviour, feelings and attitude tend to be restrictive. A creative person on the other hand will not allow these things to distract him. He will look to God to reveal His mind in a situation and give him the guidance and the wisdom to scale new heights and mountains to see beyond the problem to the solution. Therefore he will not be threatened by change. For change is adventure. Change is being able to progress; to surmount the obstacles in his way for God is with him.
Therefore keep looking out for new ways and new heights and push and push till you break through. There will be structures and persons who will resist the change but you are His instruments and in Him no one can stand the force for righteousness, change, innovation and life. Where there is life there will always be growth. Connect with people and they will follow. This is the way forward. If there is no connection then there will be resistance. So do not fear resistance or difference - rather see these as opportunities for you to grow and flower. Flower now in the place you have been planted. Sow widely and reap abundantly.

Faith in God

Faith in God - absolute trust and confidence in Him is what releases the creative forces in one to be like Him. This is God's call for you - to live as one dead - dead to the world, the devil and self - alive to God. The Holy Spirit is the one who will work in you. You are not led by circumstances but by faith in One who is above circumstances. You are led by faith to faith to move the mountains, to triumph in every circumstance because nothing can bring you down because the joy of the Lord is your strength. You will climb every mountain and believe that blessing will follow you as you face the mountains in your life. You will bring joy and gladness, solutions to intractable problems because your heart is fixed in Him. Your sights are in heaven not on earth. Therefore you see from heaven's perspective and live each day to glorify His wonderful Name. His love fills you. His Holy Spirit rejoices in you. You are One in Him. You know Him and trust Him and believe in Him therefore you are a winner.

Heavenly wisdom

Heavenly wisdom is given to the one who will believe. Believing leads to creativity. If one does not believe then where is one's hope. Believing in a God who is gracious loving and merciful. What we believe in determines our responses. If we believe in a loving and merciful God then we receive this into our hearts and in response become loving and merciful to others. On the other hand, if we believe in a God who is waving the big stick then we become like Him - ruthless and merciless to others. God in Christ laid down His life for me - so I lay down my life for others. This is the response. A heart that has not tasted and experienced God's love - fears God's wrath. Christ came to show us His way of love - not of condemnation. It's those who do not choose the road of love that feel condemned. This condemnation is not from God but from their own conscience.

Attachment to God

Attachment to God the Father means that I receive God's love into my heart. This is the healing I receive. I turn from my old beliefs to one that I have received through resurrection of Jesus Christ. I receive His love by faith. I do not fight it but like a child come to Him to receive. So Lord, I thank you. Without your mercy I am finished.

Hearing God's now voice

God sees the whole picture. If He were to see only part of the picture like I do especially in conflict and crisis then I would be condemned. I therefore can trust myself to God who leads me for He knows and sees the whole picture. I therefore need to entrust my life to Him. He is the One who is doing the work of changing me. If I listen to other voices, past and present then I will feel condemned. God wants me to hear and listen to His now voice - today speaking to me. In this way I can release myself from the past and come present to Him and to others. As long as I am stuck in the past then I recreate the past in present relationships. I cannot continue to be a victim of the past. This is a decision I have to choose. I can either allow the past to influence me or choose to live in His presence today and leave the past and the future to Him. The past and the future I have no control over. I can choose the present. It's my choices now that matter. If I choose to live in God's presence and believe in His presence and His leading and working, then I will behave in new ways that will bring healing to my past and pave a new future.

Battles

Therefore you have to submit your will to God. In this way only can you submit to others. Yet you will not submit to evil in others or in yourself. This is the battle. It is a matter of daily choices. Remember, you cannot survive for a minute without the spirit of God in you. He is the one who keeps you and looks after you. The more you are dependent on Him - the less confidence you will have in the flesh. The flesh will seek to assert itself but God's spirit when given control will subdue the flesh. These are daily choices one makes, which become habits, which then form character and finally your destiny.

Destiny

So what you are sowing now will determine your destiny. Don't be fooled that everything is okay because you know Him who purchased you with His own blood. Even the angels who rebelled were sent to hell. So be careful. The freedom in Christ does not give you license to do your own thing. You are free to live a holy life - free from the power of sin and the forces of evil. It's this freedom that enables you to live a holy life. Therefore live life to the full today for you have been freed from the powers of self, sin and Satan. Hallelujah, what a salvation. All the 3 S's vanquished through the slain blood of the Lamb - JESUS.

Jesus Christ and Him crucified

Now come into His presence - the Holy of holies made accessible to you - His child and to all His blood bought children. This is the only message the world needs to hear and see - Jesus Christ and Him crucified. See how the evil one will attack but this will drive you to abandon yourself into His arms. You don't have to struggle against sin and Satan for the moment you release yourself to Him and call upon His name - His power is released to vanquish your foes and His blood flows to cleanse, repair and to heal and restore. Jesus is alive today. His blood is living and powerful source of blessing. His Holy Spirit will come present to you. So turn your face away from sin and turn your face to God and be saved.

Satanic arrows

The glory of the Lord is upon you. See with the eyes of the spirit. See the glory like a halo around your head. Believe in this as a beloved child of God. Don't give in to the lies of the devil. He will confuse and threaten you. For every positive Word of God, he will send a counter negative word. This is the task of Satan. So don't be surprised. Faith filled words empower, energises your spirit. The negative words sent by Satan are aimed to destroy you. Be careful not to be used by Satan for his purposes - to destroy. Rather choose the narrow way of love. Yes, love is the narrow way. The way of this world is broad because it is easy; it does not require your will to commit, to choose but to flow. The way of the spirit is against the way of the world. It is a counter current that pushes back the world. Many have fallen into the trap of flowing with the world like the new age movement. This is to court with the world and the spirit of the world and in this process one is open to numerous deceiving spirits. It looks good but the end is destruction. Anything that satisfies your flesh is not of the spirit. Always judge if the underlying spirit behind the words, thoughts and actions is activated by love. If it is not, then it is of this world, the spirit of this world. Yes, there is a lot you can learn from the world but remember good or right may not be of the spirit of God. This is the danger - this is why you need discernment. Yes, people have different ways and that maybe so and right - yet on the final day God will judge through your attitude. It's your attitude that finally counts not works.

Humility

Humility is the key to access to God and power over men. This is a paradox but it is true. Men try and prove and have one over the other. Jesus came to serve. He served men so that the conflict would not be one of win/lose but of win/win. He did not lose. He took a position of humility so that others would be able to listen. No more defence. When I put others into defence then I don't relate with their real self but the false. I humble myself before God by committing all to Him. This then enables me to humble myself before men. I choose to humble myself so that my actions will enable others to relate with me not through their defences but through their real self. It is in relationship with the real that one comes to unity. Relating with the false gives one a false sense of security. It is the real that provides the life. Everything else is "maya" an illusion of the real. Defences - deceive and protect us and prevent us from coming into contact with the real. The attractiveness of distance is false till you come close and touch and feel. So people hide behind their self made castles - but they are just castles - no life in them. Real life is from within. This outward focus cannot satisfy - they are necessary but are not what leads to fulfilment. It is the contact with the real that enables one to know life. So cast out your shell of defence and come present into the real. What is real is in the relationship with the other. Relationship with God - relationship with another. One receives strength, love, hope, and joy through this relationship. The Holy Spirit in you enables you to know Him. He changes your thinking - transforms it. This transformation then leads to the emergence of the real self. The real self cannot emerge until it knows that he is loved with a perfect love. Then all fear goes and the light streams in and pushes out the darkness. The darkness of the soul keeps one blind to the real. So come to the light of Christ. His blood cleanses. His love secures. His joy propels you into action. These are all provided by the Holy Spirit. So rejoice in His cleansing. As the false gives way to the real, you come present and reach out to others to bring them into the light. The light of Christ is the salvation of man. Many walk paths to receive the light. You have the light in you. Do not be put off by the flesh. The flesh can never change - it can adjust but it is condemned to death. It is the spirit in you that lives and transforms you from the inner man. The inner man then becomes strong and rules over the outer man through the Spirit of Christ in you.

Love and humility

Humility -emptying oneself of selfish, negative and lustful desires and being submitted to God. Love - an outward directed desire to seek the best for the other are prerequisites for a closer walk with God. Without these all your desires, dreams, goals and hopes are like wind - good for now but of no eternal value. It's as you sow love that you reap a habit. It's these habits that give rise to character. These are patterns that are predictable ways of seeing and doing things. These are what make for the integrity of a person. Without these one is left empty for all one has done is build castles in the air which crumbles like paper when the winds of trials, disappointment and temptation blow. Every negative situation, thought, attitude, perception is an opportunity to sow love, to sow Kingdom values, to exercise the gifts and fruits of the Spirit, to be godly, to be light in darkness, to bring hope to desperate hearts. So you can see where this is lacking or what is built is based on short-term goals and values and these will not last.

Holy Spirit

Come to Jesus - the good Man who purchased your life by sacrificing Himself - this is the climax of character. Such a person has given His life totally to God and has no interest in this world but only in heaven. To him heaven is his home and the sooner he arrives the better and so sacrificing his life is no big deal. Let your sights also centre on God above and live each moment to the glory of His name.

God's Holy Spirit is in you so do not fear. He is so close to you that He will appear so real to you. He is like flesh and blood to you. His presence in you will be seen and heard as you live in vital union with Him. Just as Jesus was nothing so He could be something, so also it is as you live each moment in emptiness that you will be filled. New thoughts, new dreams will flow into you. When you are preoccupied with yourself then there is no place for the Holy Spirit. So empty yourself of all your own thoughts and let God fill you with His thoughts. He is in you. So you can trust Him to fill you. Be filled in the Holy Spirit. It is Jesus who baptises in the Holy Spirit. Remember His strength comes in walking in abandonment to Him. He is your strength. He is your peace. Be filled. He fills you to overflowing. He fills you as you call on His name. The Holy Spirit beckons you to come to Him. You know His voice - now as you step out of yourself, you come present to Him. He then steps into your life - taking your place. He now walks with you, talks through you, feels through you, communes with you. He is your eyes, ears, mind, and heart. He is the new owner. Your body is just a shell. A new owner - Christ's own Spirit has taken residence in you. Now do as He thinks and feels in you. See how different it feels. Your body will continue to think and feel because your body has not changed. All that has happened is that you have stepped outside so that the Holy Spirit can step in. Now He will control your thoughts, feelings and behaviour. You have His memory, His power, His wisdom, and His knowledge. You will see with His eyes, hear

with His ears, understand with His mind, and feel with His heart. Limitless, eternal, new creation - that's what you are.
Go now and act and live in this new life. What a transformation occurs as you step outside your self and let the Holy Spirit in. The old scripts that belonged to your old self now are powerless to influence you. You now move in the Spirit. It's like a new energy. See how the machine purrs in you - ready to go, to conquer the world.
One heart inspired, empowered and enlightened by God is enough to bring the world to its knees to worship the One, eternal, everlasting God. It's only a life that is prepared to leave all and follow Jesus that can live this life daily, consistently and in vital union with Him. This is not your work but God's. God works, calls, appoints and empowers the One who will be prepared to let Him come in.

Prayer power

Prayer is the most powerful weapon of a saint. This power connects your need to the resources in heaven to meet your need. It's like a bank account. When you key in the code - then money is released. Only in this case the resources in heaven are limitless. God's people can have access to His resources in heaven. They need to visualise the need, and then visualise by faith the resources in heaven, visualise the heart of the Father, and visualise Him pleading on our behalf and Jesus who has the key to unlock the door. Visualise the Holy Spirit and the angels who will deliver the gifts - healing, riches, peace, joy, all the fruits of the kingdom of God. These are obtained by earnest faith filled prayers. This is God's will. God's will is to destroy the power of sin, of Satan, of demons, of principalities and powers. God's will is to release His strength and power into His people. So now tap this power. You have got the power. Don't be limited to the scientific, sensual world where power is limited to what is seen, heard and felt. Be released into the realm of this higher power. Power to save, heal and redeem. Who has got this power? You have because you know Him and you are a blood bought child of the King of Kings - Jesus.

Prayer

Sudden inspiration that the power of positive imagination - goal setting - dreaming, is the same as prayer. This is why it works. Prayer also uses the vehicle of imagination. The key is faith in both cases. Without faith it is difficult to dream for it is in the area of believing that what is not will be. God spoke and all creation came to be. Therefore when one prays - there is a specific outcome that one believes is God's will. Prayer must be specific to achieve results. In prayer one waits till God gives the assurance - then once that assurance is received one stays with it till the request is received. Hallelujah. This is why goals are important. You become what you think and believe. Without a firm faith in God or a strong sense of purpose and trust in oneself it is difficult to dream and believe. It is all in the area of the unknown. But when one believes then anything is possible. The fruit is desire, believe, pay the price, and achieve the prize.

To be full I must be able to think freely and to do. This is only possible in Jesus - trusting in Him - to know that He is in control. It is my part to follow. I have a purpose because He goes before me. I need now to concentrate on my aptitude for in this I will flow easily and achieve great things. I cannot operate to satisfy others' wishes and desires - I need to fit in to fulfil God's desires and will. So I tune myself into the great I am and want to receive from Him direction and guidance. To hear His voice - to be led by Him - to be in constant communion with Him - to be one in Him - this is my desire and goal. To be free to do this without any fear knowing that I am loved and I will choose to be positive, enthusiastic and energetic to push back the negative forces of darkness and to operate in His light.

Visualisation

Oh, how my heart yearns to give you more than you can think or see. My people rather live by their senses and feelings than see me in the midst of their troubles. Faith sees the King - not the mountain. In the midst of the King the mountain disappears. This is what David saw when he saw Goliath. David did not fear because his King would overcome. He just threw the stone and the Holy Spirit caught it and directed it and it destroyed Goliath. We must see beyond our mountains of despair, hopelessness and fear if we are to overcome. Only a person who is moving in the positive power of God can visualise the end. Planning with the end in mind empowers you to do and be a different person.

Now visualise how you will be in heaven. This is your destination. Man plans for retirement. You plan for eternity in heaven. This is your destination. Therefore all your plans, works and desires will be empowered by this goal - to be with Jesus, to bring to Him your gifts - the things you did in His Name - the love you shared, the things you gave in His Name. All in His Name - done in His Name will be honoured for eternity. So whatever you do - remember you are a representative of Jesus. Now go in His Name and do. Confess your sins - those sins that keep tripping you up. Only do, think and say what will glorify His Name. This is your calling and service. See the joy, energy, vitality and peace that will flow as you let go and let God direct you. All your enemies will bow down and you will walk with your head high. Nothing can touch you or harm you for you are shielded and protected by the armies of heaven. Satan has no control over you. So be immersed in Him, baptised in Him, washed in Him, filled in Him.

Faith

Faith is God's door to receiving. It is through the door of faith that you have access to the treasures in heaven. Faith is the door to combat all the fear and negativity in this world. Faith in God - Father, Son and Holy Spirit - a personal God - gives you the object of your faith. Now when you put your trust and faith in Him then you open other doors through faith. Windows of opportunity are opened to you. So you have one order in the flesh - the way you work and see the world and operate in the world. With the other set you see the things in the spiritual by faith. Faith is the key to bring the two parts of yourself into union.

Holy Spirit the conductor

The Holy Spirit is the connection. So when you walk in the Spirit and let Him control your life then He will bring your spirit life in union with your flesh life and see what a combination you have. For this, the self has to die. This is also done by faith. You get your energy through your faith life. You implant through your flesh life. So you see that the two can work together but the conductor must be the Holy Spirit.

When you operate in the Spirit it is as if it is in the heavenlies but has no earthly meaning. In the flesh you see results of order and work with diligence. However for the work on earth to have the quality of life it needs to be infused with life from heaven. This is what faith does.

Faith is the language of the heart. Feelings communicate to the state of your heart. By faith you can overcome the negative images and feelings of the heart. Your faith is in the positive power of God who will release this positive love, faith, hope, joy, and peace to you as long as you focus on Him.

So you have both worlds open to you. You must choose who your Master will be. The choice will determine the outcome of your life. This is a daily choice, a minute by minute choice. Only a life in Him will have the qualities that lead to a productive, vibrant and exciting life. Routine work based on earthly ways of thinking and doing will exhaust itself through age and boredom. However, the life of heaven is eternal. It never ends. It goes on and on and on. So don't lose courage. Tune into the Spirit today and be encouraged and inspired and empowered. Your faith will see you through to the end just as it did the saints before. Keep working, hoping and living life to the full in the Spirit.

The Spirit life is the life of heaven. This heavenly life is what you need to bring into your dealings on earth. It will bring the other side of your nature - God created nature into being. Now don't separate it off. It needs to come present in all your dealings. In this way you will be able to integrate both sides of your being ie. spirit, soul and body. The body will follow the urging's of the spirit and soul.

Imagination

Your imagination is fired by faith. This then fires your feelings, which then influences your thinking processes. Your mind then implements the outcome of your imagination, feelings and thinking. Faith imagination, inspired by the spirit will bring a unity and synchrony into your life that will cause others to flow in the same way. So keep your eyes on Jesus the author and perfector of your faith and live life to the full knowing that you are in the palm of His hand and nothing can take away the joy and peace you enjoy of His life in you.

Faith imagination

Firing up on goals, vision, imagination, and faith imagination as the vehicle to success or accomplishment of goals and dreams. So have to have the prize or goal clearly fixed in the imagination - then see it each day till it is received. Thank you God. This is a venture with God - so I will just be led by Him. In this is perfect peace. At all times I will trust Him. He never fails. This is it - faith to conquer every fear. Without faith there is no hope. With no hope - the heart will lose courage and therefore attract defeat, disease and hurt. This is why a strong faith is a protection against all negativity - words, bugs, and accidents. Wow! The peace of God, which is a result of trust in God, so anaesthetises you to the negative influence that you can fly like an eagle. Positive faith results in possibilities and solutions leading to victory in all areas of my life.

Love

This is love - wanting to do for others, to bless others, to give and be a blessing, source of hope. When hope and faith dies - love dies. Faith, hope and love. Love then inspires faith and hope. These 3 remain when all else disappears. So finally it is love that counts. So help me to love O Lord. To bless others.

When I withdraw then I stop loving.

Love does not pick or choose. Love gives no matter what. Love loves her enemies. How great love is this.

I love by being a emblem of His love. How? By being continuously filled in the Holy Spirit. How? By moving in Him - in His gifts and fruits. These are a product of the in filling. I can't make it up. It just flows. It is only when I am connected to Him is this possible. I connect with him. He connects with me. As fuel is poured in - so power is released for love is to be shared. I will imagine that I am connected to Gods fuel pump. He fills me up. The pistons fire off the engines of my heart and mind giving direction to my love. It is His love through me. Others will feel it, experience it as they come in contact with me.

The main area of conflict is in the area of your soul. Your soul has been tutored on experiences and influences that are related to past relationships. This all needs to be handed over to Christ the Healer. He will change those patterns as each reaction is offered up to Him. The flesh will only change when it suffers. Everything in this age is directed to alleviate the suffering to the flesh. This is why materialism and existentialism conspire to keep the person from the realities of sin and death. It's only in suffering that the flesh will die. All self-centredness is geared to soften the blow to the flesh. All defences are directed to preserve the flesh. This is why only identification with the Son is the only way out of the flesh into the spirit. Old patterns will then be changed. The fullness of the Spirit will bring His joy and peace and love that will create Christ like responses, which will melt hearts. The heart only understands the language of love. Agape love strikes deep into the heart and lowers the defences. Therefore choose to operate in love in all circumstances. The devil hates love. He sows hatred. Only love can win the battle. Whatever other faults a man may have - no one can fault a man for loving. So choose to love at all times. Do not think of your own pleasures but of others. When you choose to love then others will want to be with you. So now live only for Christ and others.

Love is above difference

The Lord impressed on me how people are more important than our differences. Love is what makes a difference in times of conflict. It is the one who knows how to love that makes the difference in the outcome of the difference. Difference will always be there - what we do with the difference is what is important. If I allow the negative forces of difference to move me away then I will move away but if I convert it into a positive force to invigorate, challenge and bring forth a third solution then I become a creative force. Lord, come and help me to channel the energy of difference into a positive force that will enable me to overcome all negativity and bring peace. This is what Jesus did. He came into the world as a positive force overcoming the negativity of sins and bringing in His peace.

Investing in others

Investing in others is to give away part of Christ in me. Christ came to give. So when I initiate loving actions I partake of this giving. Suffering comes from love not being received - Christ continues to suffer through His people who extend His love to others and are rejected. Only love can win hard, cold, defensive hearts. There is no other way.

Victorious living

Everything is a process. I am constantly changing, evolving, maturing as I walk by faith. Routine and fear keep me stuck. Faith and belief are opposite to routine and the general grind. I live by faith daily so I can expect new revelations, new insights, new levels of achievement, surprises, rewards as I move forward by faith. Faith is the key to moving mountains. The mountains (problems, situations, blocks) are there to enable us to exercise faith. Faith sees that finally I will win - victory is mine. Victory maybe in the form of experience, knowledge, expertise but victory is sure. Failure is not defeat but the stepping stone to success. The ying and yang, positive and negative are always around. When I choose faith, I choose the positive. Without faith a man cannot be victorious. He is dependent on his own skills, own talents, and own choices. In God, by faith, one is safe because one is dependent on God. This is the shift that occurs. So I will just flow - knowing what is right to do and as I put my hands to the plough I know that He will give me the strength to do, to achieve, to purchase what I desire. My heart's desire is to achieve His purposes for my life. Therefore I choose to die to my own selfish desires and to live according to His will. His plan for my life is far greater than any plan I have. His way is better, for His way leads to eternity. My way is so short sighted. I live for Jesus. I live for Him, my Creator and my God. I have an open channel with Him. I will wait in the land. His spirit will rejoice in me. He will give me joy, peace, strength. His angels will guard over me. He will be my joy and crown. So I will bless the Lord continuously. I will rejoice in the Lord. I will accept others.

Difference is not opposition. Difference is variety, is color, and is abundant living. I will capitalize on difference. More than what people say or do is to know that they are all created in Gods image. Therefore, I will love them and be salt to them - light, peace and love. With this attitude I can make a difference in their lives. I will seek to serve and bless for this is my calling. I will take up my cross daily - for in this is my salvation. I believe in Jesus. I believe in life after death. I believe in me - because He lives in me. I will operate in the power of my new name. I am, therefore I can, I will, I believe.

Bondage

To be Christ is to influence your surroundings. When you find yourself becoming defensive that's when all other thoughts will assail you. This is why it is so important to be dead to self. Self when on the throne thinks defensively. When thinking defensively, then you are at the mercy of the influences around you - mainly negative. To be under the influence of others is to be operating in fear. You become self-conscious. You freeze up. All your faculties become constricted. You become bound and not free. This is bondage. You have

subjected yourself to the spirit of this world.
In Christ - your self is crucified. You operate from the spirit in you. You are influenced from within. You can then influence your circumstances. You operate freely. Not bound by the spirit of this world. You are not called to be of this world. You are called to be in this world. The Holy Spirit in you controls your feelings and thoughts. You are not ruled by your senses. Your spirit is surrounded by Gods' Spirit. He influences your feelings and thoughts.

God is in control

You acknowledge that God is in control. You therefore submit all to Him and follow His leading. You operate in the gifts and fruits of the Spirit. In this way you push back the forces of darkness and bring light into the situation. Whatever you do or say, do it in the fullness of the Holy Spirit. Relaxed in mind and body you minister into the spirit of man. It's not through human understanding but through revelation that men are convicted of their sin. That is why man can hear and not understand and see and not perceive. When the Holy Spirit speaks then He speaks to the spirit man - that part of man that is created in the image of God that is marred by sin. It is His breath that will bring life to this spirit of man that has been cut off by the blindness of sin. When the light of God's word spoken in the Holy Ghost shines on him then the blindness is removed and God shines into him. His secret thoughts and intentions of the heart are laid bare. He is convicted, repents and receives cleansing.
So strive to enter into the holy of holies. This striving is of the spirit. This is to enter into the place where you will operate in true freedom - not in the fear of man but of God.

Creator God

The purpose of living, of life, is to glorify your Creator. What the fall brought about was an ignorance of the Creator God. What new birth brought back was the realisation and experience of Creator God. Now the Kingdom of God is in existence to those who have experienced His salvation. Many seek for a salvation that will bring release, meaning and hope but fail to know their Creator. This knowledge of Creator God can only be experienced through a personal relationship with Him. This is possible through God's Holy Spirit who was sent to earth to be born in individuals who put their trust and faith in the death and resurrection of Jesus Christ – God's Son. Jesus identified with the fallen state of man so that He could lead men to experience His salvation purchased for men through the shedding of His blood. This is the heavenly exchange that took place 2000 years ago to reclaim lost humanity. Now all creation can wait expectantly for total deliverance from sickness, pain and death when Jesus returns in all His glory to claim His inheritance. This is the gospel of Jesus Christ.

Prayer of renunciation

Now in response to this great salvation, I respond in eternal gratefulness. I say Lord; I come to you naked - clothe me. I come to you empty - fill me. I come to you an orphan - posses me as your son into your family. I come to you broken - heal me of all my diseases and set me free. I come to you lonely - fill me and comfort me. I come to you a sinner - save me. I come to you unclean - cleanse me in your blood. Wash me and clothe me. Lord, you have done all for me. I come now to offer my body as a living sacrifice wholly and totally surrendered to you - to do as you will to glorify your lovely name.

Gratefulness

Gratefulness - response of the human heart to the love of God. A grateful heart will always respond in love for there is nothing that can harden such a heart. A grateful heart knows the price that was paid - Jesus death on the cross. This is the vision that the heart needs to capture to respond in gratefulness. I am indebted to my Lord for His death. Nothing else matters as I look to Him for every need. He supplies to me out of His abundance. When I walk in the Spirit then He fills me to overflowing and I respond in gratefulness. I am a sinner - I am still prone to sin - I am still in the flesh. I am prone to temptation and therefore to sin. Yet I am born again - born of the Spirit and therefore I have God in me in the person of the Holy Spirit. God reveals His will to me as I walk in the spirit. In the spirit I come present to God - I am and therefore I have a being, I come present to Him. I live in the mighty presence of God. I live to show forth His glory. He shines through me. I realise it is through His grace. People are affected by His spirit in me. They are not convinced by strong arguments. Rather their attention is caught by what they see and feel. This is why no amount of reasoning has any effect. One is touched by belief, meaning and feeling. In families such beliefs are handed down and despite contrary evidence no change occurs. This is a form of 'brain washing'. Meaning is in the belief. Belief is central to ones' being. Without meaning one is but a composite of matter. It is meaning that gives humans a desire to live. Therefore someone who desires to live a life of holiness needs to live "in" God - be filled in His Spirit - die to his own desires and live in the freedom of the Spirit.

The Spirit brings in His love to infill the heart. His love crosses all natural boundaries. Satan is against this. Satan is the opposite of love - indifference. This is what we see in the world - a spirit of indifference. There is no care - for there is no meaning. It is only people with vision, with hope, with faith can be a source of power to people who live lives full of despair and hopelessness. Only people of God have a hope that can inspire faith and bring forth the love of God. Faith in God brings hope and love. Love is the desperate need of every human being. This can only be satisfied through a personal relationship with the Saviour. Such a love is Gods' kind of love. It is not an earthly kind of love that is here today and gone tomorrow. God's love is of substance. It never fails.

Self sacrifice

Self-sacrifice is the theme of the Christian faith. This is the life principle of Jesus Christ. He came to sacrifice His life that I may live. His example will be the life principle of every behaviour. It's only when this life principle is made a priority in the life of the believer that power can be released from on high to empower the believer to live in heavenly power. This is what moved the stone. Jesus died - choosing to die the death of a slave rather than hold on to his position of God. This is the attitude you need to have. Knowing His love and salvation. I die that others may live. As long as I hold on to what is dear to me I will not be able to give. It's in sacrifice that others may be blessed. This attitude needs to prevail over your life. Others give of their abundance. This is not sacrifice. Only a willing sacrifice is pleasing to God. God's love enshrined in one's heart moves a person to sacrifice knowing that it is only in this way that more of God's love can flow into one's heart. Mother Theresa operated on this principle. She gave knowing that God would provide. Every need that comes my way will be my opportunity to give. This then sets in progress a wheel of giving that does not stand still but rolls to gather more in the way of giving. It is a spiritual principle. Life comes as self will dies and God's spirit is released. Spirit of love, peace and patience. I die to self-love - releasing God's love through me. I die to impatience that God's patience is released through me. I die to unrest that Gods' peace may flow through me. I die to my own sense of ability that Gods' gifts may be produced in me. When God is no.1 then all this will flow as a response. God's positives for my negatives. So I don't defend my negatives but I boast of my negatives that God's love may pervade me. Holding on to negatives is like poisoning myself. This breeds self-hatred. I therefore release my hurts and resentments so that God can come in and free me from fear power. I release them to God. I say Lord take them. I release my burden to you. You carry it. You went to the cross for this purpose.

Yoked to Christ

Jesus said take my yolk upon you. I am yoked together with you. I don't carry the burden on my own. Just as two bullocks are yoked together to plough the field so also I am yoked to Christ. Now I follow His leading. My burden is light because

He carries it. I am just so grateful. I release my burdens to Him. Now I am free to live in His presence to do His will. I don't have to worry about my burden. I live in the abundance of His love and joy. I live to follow Him. All I do I will do to the best of my ability because Gods' strength inspires me. I attempt for excellence because Christ's mighty energy propels me.

Abundant living

Faith is the confident assurance of things not seen, the certainty that what we hope for we will receive even though we do not see it ahead. Salvation, hope, faith. What more can I ask - with so many gone ahead - suffered, overcome, what more do I need but to trust in God to overcome in His name - promises that I have now and receive through faith - nothing is impossible - bringing God's plan, ideas, into being on earth - incarnation. Jesus, incarnation of God - so also what we imagine – God's ideas become incarnate as I walk in faith. Such faith challenges and inspires others - brings conviction, brings hope, excites others - this is what faith does - not limited by the material world or senses - it is to do with the inner eyes. God has spoken His Word - you have obtained the promise - now walk in it - be positive - others will benefit as you enlarge your heart.
God has called me to have abundant life. The faith challenge is to break through this barrier - God does this through ideas. When I look to God - He will give me the idea that will attract someone. This is how discoveries have been made. There is so much to discover - a man who trusts God can break through - for Gods' idea will enable him to breakthrough.
If I am enjoying something then I can by faith rest my body by praying in tongues - releasing endorphins, stimulants. One does not need drugs to do this - faith in God is the key. The Cross, the symbol of our salvation from all negativity - cancels out and brings in His love, peace and restoration. So in all areas I can educate my brain to not give in to the flesh but to rise up. Every addiction, habit, weakness can be broken in the Name of Jesus (object) of my faith.

Only positive attitude and stance can lead to balance. There is negativity all around and only the positive power of God can cancel these negative vibes from the environment. A man needs to put his trust in the positive power of God. The concept of destiny is vital to this - as when I know I am going to be with Jesus then nothing matters for this thought will hold me. Everything else is secondary - to meet ones own ego needs. However when I know how useful a gift is or a work is or goods are, then I will want to sell it. So despite the negative reactions one continues to sell the product one believes in. This is what is required. If there is no belief in the product - then one undersells oneself from the start. I believe in Jesus and therefore I want to sell Him to others - not because I will get points but because I am thinking of the good of the other. Jesus came to save sinners.

Trust in God

When circumstances are allowed to influence you then you will go up and down. This is why you need to be walking in the Spirit. Then the assurance and trust you have in the Lord is what will sustain you. Circumstances, situations will change but the God who never changes will keep you. He is always there - even in the darkest moment. So trust in Him. This is where you receive strength. Joy comes from within. So as you grow from within what comes from without is a gift, extra. Building the kingdom from within for the Kingdom of God is within you. So the trials, tests and tribulations are to enable you to grow in strength. Trust in God will enable you to do this. Faith in His word will be the source of strength. His word is the living Word. Only faith can make it a living word. rhema word to you. Your emotions will respond to what you put your trust in. If it is in God then your feelings will be under your control. If it is in the external then your feelings will be dictated by the happenings. So the way to function is to be in tune with the Holy Spirit - this is true freedom- freedom to make choices. I choose how I will behave, respond in every situation. I choose today to walk by faith. My tomorrow is in God's hand - I choose to be and therefore I will. So help me

Lord to grow in strength.

Moving in faith

Resting in Him is to flow in faith. Flowing in faith is to move forward - moving forward is to experience change - change in the present, future and past. For as my present changes it becomes a changed past. So onwards, upward and outward I march each day, knowing that each day I face new challenges and new victories. I shall work, learn and love as long as I have breath. I will not be stuck by rules and regulations. These are for children. Rather I shall rise up and gain new ground. I shall mount up on wings like an eagle. I shall see the Lord with God's eyes. I shall not be shaken by minor troubles, present disappointments but fix my eyes on the goal.
It is love - this is what will enable people to change, to take risks and try. Without love people are straightjacketed and manipulate others to meet their need. In this, they are always dependent on others and therefore fears and lies will rule and ruin their lives. True security is inward. So I trust in Him who lives in me and now I am able to step out of my false self - like breaking out of my grave through resurrection power and walk in resurrection power.
Praising Him is the way forward. Praise - releases faith - releases the fruits and gifts of the Spirit - fills you up to believe leading to action. Visions, dreams, thoughts are the product of a man who moves in faith - who is filled in the Spirit. Filled in the Spirit - walking in the Spirit is the goal each day of your Christian walk. Now you know that nothing in you is sufficient to cope or operate or function effectively each day. Without the Spirit you are but an empty shell. To live life on the edge you need the Spirit of God. Faith in what? Faith in God who enables you to believe to achieve. This is possible, as you trust the Lord to lead you. He will bring the opportunities to you. Do not despair during times of quiet - the Spirit is at work. Keep the goal always in mind. Don't let that vision dim. It is focus on the dream/goal that leads to achievement. Things that are not seen are seen - impossible becomes possible. This is the walk of faith. So don't fret and worry or be anxious for these

are anti faith - based on unbelief. You have to break through these barriers - how - by praising Him. Praising Him means seeing the results by faith before they happen. In this state of mind and spirit you will move towards the goal. Anything else leads to regression. With the goal in mind then you will be able to overcome all hindrances. See how the mind focused on the goal will prepare itself for all obstacles. You have to overcome the obstacles to reach the goal. Don't give up. Let the vision of freedom so empower and energise you. Then you will look back and see the victories on the way. So release and commit all to God. This is all training on the way and is solution focused. This requires a shift from a mind set trained to pick up pathology to a mindset based on faith - to see problems solved. The 2 are different mindsets. One is based on pathology. Treatment is based on solutions to the pathology. However, when one is too focused on pathology it's difficult to shift to a state of solution. However when one is in a solution-focused state, one starts with the positives, which shifts the emphasis and moves the negatives. Flush out the negatives so that the positive can take it's place. The negative influences have to go. Jesus is a positive influence because on the Cross He dealt a deadly blow on all the negatives. He crossed them out. Faith in the blood of the Cross releases you from all negatives - spiritual, emotional and physical. Now you are cleansed and free. Faith in this releases you from the negatives. Now faith in the resurrection power delivers you from these negative influences. One to cross out and cancel - the other to deliver. Deliverance means freedom from fear. Negatives cause fear. Positive power of God expels it out. Once you live in the resurrection power then no negatives can assail you. This is it. Pentecost was the induement in power - Gods' resurrection power. Now no negative could stand in the way. Resurrection power released the disciples from all fear. They were changed from weak, fearful people. Look forward - not backward. You need faith only to live today not yesterday. Faith in the Cross will take care of your yesterdays.
Positive state of mind leads to change.

Walking in the spirit

The difference between a man of faith and an unbeliever is that the man of faith will have a positive outlook on life. He is on an adventure. Everyday he looks to God to help him be a light, a source of peace and joy to others. This is the way a man of faith operates - in complete trust and faith in God. He does not listen to his flesh but to His Spirit. He sows in the Spirit and reaps in the Spirit. This evidence will be seen in the flesh. Jesus prayed but He also healed and fed and clothed. Gods Spirit is above the material realm. A man of God has to by faith penetrate the Holy of Holies to receive the things of God. This is only possible in the Spirit. It is in the Spirit that a man receives vision and a mission.

Success comes to those that believe in success. Success is always there for those who trust and believe in it. Because of the positive outlook, positive results are obtained. Don't be put off by failure. See it as a stepping stone to success. Believe, receive and achieve success. This is the law of the Spirit - as you believe - faith will push back the barrier as you break through to the promised land.

Faith walk

God will supply all you need - resources, energy, knowledge, wisdom, as you trust in Him. Moses was called out - he complained but all he got was to trust in the Lord. So also your life is a walk of faith- trusting in the Lord- this is the only way to move forward. The false security of status, job, position, family and friends will not be able to sustain you on the day of reckoning. Only trust and faith in God. All the men of faith trusted God. Lydia trusted God. Ruth trusted God. You are called to be different. You are called to be a saint. You have one life. Give it all you got. It's not what others think but what you think that is important. Stick to that. Operate in what you feel and think. This is what matters. This will bring a congruence in your walk and talk. This is what will build you up. This is integrity.

Faith is the key. Faith is only needed when I have left everything and have to trust in God alone. When my feet is off the bed of the sea, when I am off the ground, when I have stepped out into the troubled waters then I begin to operate not in the known but unknown. God has called you not to walk into the unknown alone. This is where you will need to trust God for all your resources. This is exciting and exuberating and liberating. Now you do not walk by sight but by faith. This releases a higher potential within you. This is what you need to challenge you to higher levels of performance. The known becomes so ordinary, mundane, routine. Now step out at work too in faith. Work from within. Don't be put off by voices that pull you to keep to the norm. Rather step out to challenge the system. The system cages you in. Be bold, be innovative, extraordinary. This is the way to super success. This is revolutionary thinking. This is change. Change comes as I step out in faith and release myself to Almighty God. He is my Alpha and Omega, in Him I will trust. I will trust in Him. I will cleanse myself and release myself from all other sins and trust in Him. He will lead me and guide me -step by step till I reach the place of complete surrender. I will operate in wisdom at all times. I will operate in love at all times. I will be one - united with my Lord. His love will so flow and overflow through me. I will be a banner for the Lord- witnessing to His grace, mercy and love - His compassion, glory and deliverance.

Walking with Jesus

The why is more important than the how. Why am I doing this?
Jesus knew why therefore He sanctified Himself daily so that sin would not have power over Him. Whenever self is in rule - sin has an opportunity. It is self that is on the cross - take up your cross daily that has power over sin. I am crucified with Christ. Why? So that I too can have the power of God in me to overcome and fulfil Gods mission. It is in this that I become His warrior. I just do as He commands. He will lead me step by step. He will give me His vision, which will become my

mission, which then will give me the power to do. I will listen to His voice, which will lead me, encourage me and strengthen me. Peter heard Jesus voice and he stepped out and walked on water. So also God will give me His faith when I require it to walk on the water - to expect the impossible. So help me Lord in my walk. I look to the Lord so am open to opportunities all the time. He will put His thoughts into my mind.

A dream, which is not involving the improvement, investment and betterment of others, will not have the power to change, to revolutionise. This requires faith.

Giving till it hurts

Giving is the only way. Give till it hurts. It is easy to give when it doesn't hurt. True giving is an attitude of the heart. Christ gave till he went to the Cross. Then He attained resurrection power. A heart that knows love learns to give. Giving becomes automatic. A heart that is starved of love cannot give - it just takes. Faith in action is love. Love in action is service. Faith in God learns to receive from God and gives back to God. One must have faith in something. One must believe. God has revealed Himself in Jesus Christ. Jesus Christ stands offering His life, His blood to all those who will put their trust and faith in Him. So when one puts His trust and faith in Jesus - power is released to cleanse and make whole. Sin's power is cut and Gods power is released into the life. Now life is brought forth - then from then on it is a walk of faith, by faith in the Lord Jesus Christ. Jesus through His Holy Spirit communicates Gods desires, intentions to the soul that waits on him. God nurtures and purifies the soul till he is made whole.

Breaking through

The Christian walks each day believing that God has His plan for his life. Each day I live as if it is the last day I have to share His love. He pours His love into my heart. He heals and restores my soul. I live each day praising His name. I leave all to Him. He deals with all the negative thoughts and feelings as I commit all to Him. This is an act of faith as well as I leave all at His feet. I commit myself to Him. I live each day seeking His face. I am secure in Him. Therefore, I will not give in to the pressures from without. I must stay true to what I believe. This is the only way to break through. God will take me through the pain as I keep my focus on Him. I need to bear my own cross. It is only in this way that resurrection power will come forth. I need to die to all that is of self. When I choose righteousness then I choose to walk the straight and narrow way. In all this my attitude is to stand for right, to be upright, patient, kind, loving, thoughtful, sensitive and empathic. All these positive fruits will come forth as I die to self and consecrate my life to Him.

Clear conviction leads to clear expectation, Gods' promises - His will - knowing this leads to clear conviction - expectation that God will answer. If I know what is Gods will then I can expect His will to be done because Gods law always follows. The wicked flourish when the righteous sit back and do nothing. It is opposing evil that is required. Evil will only be pushed back when men of God stand and speak.

Speaking God's truth in love

Sin is a reality. Sin has to be confronted - brought into the light. How? When you speak for the truth. Remember God and His angels are always behind you. You are called to walk forward. The angels will protect you. Then the Holy Spirit will lead you. He will go before you but only when you move forward. He cannot lead unless you take the step of faith. Taking the step of faith releases Gods power. Gods power is only required for the impossible task. What is possible is for you to do. But if God wants you to go beyond yourself, you must be prepared to walk by faith. Any mountain can be brought low.

Faith in self in God

It is not faith in self - but faith in God. This is where the conflict lies. One believes that faith in oneself is anti faith in God. This is not true. God builds, sanctifies, polishes, and refines so that I can be strong. So belief that I can do it reinforces faith in God and vice versa. If one is dependent in ones efforts then God is not required. But if faith demands confidence in God which then translates into experience and the self is built up. It is the sinful self that needs to die - for it is self seeking. The righteous self is possessed by Christ and needs to be built up. So I know that all selfish, devious, jealous, proud and egotistical tendencies belong to the old-nature. The old nature is cancelled but because of habit patterns of a lifetime - those effects are still around in the flesh. It is these effects that need to be changed through the mighty power of the Holy Spirit. So I will look to God. I will stand in truth. I will love fully. I will wait for the opportune time. I will stand against all pride and the force of evil that will work against Gods children. I know the truth - so as I speak it forth the blindness will be lifted. God's truth is anti the wisdom of man. What is the wisdom of man? It is based on carnal knowledge. This is where discernment is required. God is calling for a holy people to stand against the forces of evil. Will you stand for God? Will you speak forth for righteousness. Yes, Lord I will. Then die to self - this is the only way. I believe and therefore I shall speak. Don't be afraid of resistance. Stand - just stand there and face the enemy. He will flee from you as you stand. Why? Because just as a dog will run after you if you run, so Satan will run after you if you run. But if you stand then Satan will back off. Only fools run. The righteous will stand. So stand on the Word of God and the promises of God.

Vision

Without a vision, other people's plans will be imposed on us. This is so important as to be sure as to what ones own vision is. It is so easy to forget our own visions and let someone else's plans determine our future. This is like being sold off to slavery. So keep your vision in mind for this is the only way to win - to move forward in faith. Without a vision the people perish. Outside forces will come and go but it is only a people of vision that will stand and rise.

Experiences come and go but it is faith and trust in the Lord who you do not see that counts. Experience without faith and trust will not last. They are like vapour that comes and goes. Trust - that solid quality that lasts is what you need to develop. The Holy Spirit gifts you with faith - faith releases the gifts because it trusts in God who is the giver. In Jesus Name you have faith that can move mountains. Everything that will stand in your way will move as you put your trust in Him. He is ever present. God seeks to bless all who will trust in Him. His love enriches you and you can depend on Him to save you and help you.

Sanctifying our bodies daily for the Holy Spirit

The Holy Spirit comes to possess the body - just as Jesus came in the body as a sacrificial offering so that we may have the experience of the indwelling spirit. The Holy Spirit has come to indwell man and is possible only because Jesus offered up His place in heaven so that He could make the way for us. Without this offering of Himself it would not have been possible. His sacrifice made it possible - so now we in turn are called to sacrifice our bodies as a living sacrifice daily for the possession of the Holy Spirit. No sacrifice - no power. This is a daily process of dying and living - dying to self - living in Christ. The new birth is a dying to the old life and the reception of the new life. Only those who are in Christ are able to do this. Without Him it is impossible to live the Christian life of holiness, purity and love. These are all spiritual attributes. In Him alone is there life and this life, eternal. In Him we have the joy and the power. It is not dependent on others, circumstances or influences but on the Spirit. Only in the Spirit can you be. So trust Him to enable you to be - to become a new person in Christ.

Overcoming faith

Lord, what is life but a whisper - born today - gone tomorrow. Each day is a new day - the past is gone forever - a memory. Don't let the memory spoil your today. Today is like a new day

- as if there was no yesterday. Today live as if there is no tomorrow - to the full - what would you do? I will live in the joy of the Lord. Tomorrow is the Lords. I will be a witness to His power. When past hurts - fears emerge, I will say I don't know what that is about - I have committed it to the Lord - I have been washed and cleansed in the blood. I am clean - I abide in Him. The fullness of the Spirit is in me as I abide in Him. I live each day in what is, by faith. I live each moment by faith expecting the best. Hallelujah, I am free as long as I have breath, I will expect the best. By faith I am redeemed by faith. All I have is by faith. So Lord, create in me a clean heart that I can see into the spirituals and give birth in the physical. It is these things that count and therefore I will rejoice. I will commit all things to the Lord for He is the One who loves me and by His grace and mercy He has seen me this far. Blessed is the name of the Lord. Only the Lord can truly satisfy. Even in down times it is He alone who is able to see me through to the end. So my dignity and personhood is found in Him. Each man needs to seek and he will find. It is a persons self worth - meaning, purpose, that makes him.

Discerning the spirit

The spirit that controls the family determines the atmosphere in the family. This spirit is usually through the head. If the head gives in then the dominant spirit of the woman takes over. If there is strife it is because there is conflict between the man and the woman. So only a spirit of love in the head can give rise to a submissive spirit or arouse the submissive spirit in the woman. So seek to love, to serve, to lead by example - then the rest of the body will follow. Jesus is the example. When I am submitted to Him I will lead by example. Abiding in Him means to be submitted to His Spirit. His Holy Spirit in you will lead you each step of the way. You need to submit to Him. Influences around you will be there but it is the dominant spirit that will guide your thinking and doing. This is the only way to overcome. Otherwise you will always be influenced by your environment. When you operate from your true centre then you will always be at peace. Do not be controlled by the spirits of others but overcome by faith each obstacle. It is who you are in the Spirit that matters. Don't be anxious to lead - be yourself and others will naturally look to you. In the end it is not whether you lead or not, but are true to yourself. Believe in yourself. Believe in the Spirit within you. This integrity is what will make you feel alive. Otherwise you are like a robot with no soul. It is the soul of man that determines who he is. Others will have different spirits controlling them. Be true to the Holy Spirit within you. Be honourable. Do not be overcome but stand in the midst of conflict. Pray in the Spirit. No one can overpower you as long as you stand in the Spirit. It's not what others say and think about you but what you say and think about yourself that matters. So be steadfast as a rock because Christ the Rock, lives in you. Stay true and be encouraged.

Values

Ask, believe, receive - this is the way forward in the Christian life. To persevere. Whatever you allow your mind to feed on will occupy your mind. So occupy your mind with things of the spirit - with the things that will sustain you in hard times. The true character of the soul is seen in the hard times when troubles come and the resources of the soul are then evident. When the resources of the flesh and the world are insufficient to sustain you then you have to rely on the resources of the soul. What are they? The resources of the soul are based on values - on love, goodness, and faithfulness. These values are eternal. One sees the true character of the soul when trouble comes or one loses the things that are so precious in the world. This is when one's true allegiance is seen - to God above or to the material resources of the earth. When Israel received miracles - they were pleased but in trouble they complained. They worshipped the Lord with their mouths but not with their hearts. Therefore, their true character was seen. It is in the daily walk that you are seen for what you really are. It is in the quiet moment that who you are is revealed. Man occupies himself with things. What happens when these things are removed? Is there any meaning left? A true and effective indication of a mans soul is to know how he is operating now. If he is walking in faith, in joy then he is right in his soul. If he is looking to go and escape from his troubles then he is not walking in faith but in fear. Faith expects the best - hopes for the best - believes in the best.

Choices

Everyone has to fit to a plan, but the responsive person is able to change, to adjust his priorities. It is prioritizing that enables a person to choose each day what is important. What is the next step. So have plans, goals but also be prepared to adjust. However in this don't waste time. Prioritizing means to choose - not just follow the crowd. For following the crowd doesn't get you anywhere. So at the end of the day you have to make the choices after having considered the alternatives. I cannot make another to do - I can only ask. When I am in a relationship then others will want to do what I ask - will want to serve - will want to help.

Christ in me

Christ is God. In Him I have everything. He dwells in me and His indwelling presence enables me to be a conqueror. Christ is the One who enables me to do and to be a conqueror. I am not defeated. I am learning how to walk with God. Life presents many challenges - I learn each day how to overcome in the Spirit. I am one with him. He is in me and He enables me to conquer through his Spirit in me. I am one with Him and I am able to do all things in Christ who is able to help me to do it. All I need to do is decide and His power is released through me. Nothing can assail me unless I allow it to overcome me. I am able to love and to defend and to do all that Christ has called me to do. He will enable me to do this. I can do it. He is able to help me to do it. I have all I need. All power is given to me because Christ said it and He indwells me so I can say it. I just need to trust him. I am able to break every barrier that will keep me limited to the physical realm. I just need to relax. I need to get out of the zone of mere human endeavour. I need to seek the supernatural in all areas. It is His supernatural power that is available to me to overcome.

Prophetic word

This is the secret I reveal to you today. In your weakness you will find strength. This is my strength. Man tries to build Himself up and will fall for he builds a defence and so becomes blind to the obvious. He rejects Me for the theories and opinions of men. So be humble - learn from Me and be wise. Then from the simple things like the ants and the examples of men of God who did great things in My strength and in My Name - learn. Humility comes through the knowledge that you have received all knowledge, power and wisdom from Me. Therefore, resist the temptation to laud it over others. Rather seek to empty yourself of all preconceived, ideas, judgments, biases and perceptions and learn from the now. Be prepared to be foolish to be wise. Pretence is a defence - just like fantasy. Don't be led by the image but real. In this way you become like the real. The real is in you - Christ in you the hope of glory. Trust Him in you and live life to the full today. All things are possible to him who trusts and never relents. Persist in the faith you know and riches will come to you from heaven above.

Changed into His image

The perfect will of God for you is to be content in what you are, whom you have, where you are and what you are doing. God will show you the next step. But where you are now is where God wants you to be and to shine in the midst. This is Gods calling for you. He will move you at the right time. God is not concerned about what you have - He is more concerned about changing you into the image of Jesus. This was the reason for His coming - to leave on earth a body of people who will be light and salt in a fallen world. This is your calling - you can either build on the outside - wealth and security that will not be able to bring you any peace of mind till you know Him.

Death brings life into focus

You see life is an illusion till it is confronted with death. It is the reality of death that brings life into focus - and the meaning of life. Without death in the equation of life - life is just a dream - here today and gone tomorrow. Death is the driving force in life. For the quality of life you live is only related to the appreciation of the finality of death. There is nothing as final as death of the body. It is in the body that you make decisions for eternal life or death. So rejoice that you know life for it is your new life in the Spirit that will enable you to face death daily. For to die is beautiful as it is the passage to eternal glory. Now you know the glory is revealed in His Son Jesus through the Holy Spirit. The Holy Spirit in you lives forever. He is at work in you to prepare you for death and an entrance into life everlasting. So don't concern yourself with things of the flesh - for they are all doomed to die. Why invest in something that is going to perish. Rather invest in things eternal - these are the spiritual values of love, joy, peace, patience, wisdom and knowledge that lasts forever. No one can take this away from you. Time is no more measured in minutes and days and years - it is eternal. So you live each day and the Lord provides and blesses as you sow the seeds of eternal life. The blessings you receive on earth are just droppings compared with what is happening within you. It is what happens within you that will translate into things that will be perceived and received without. Therefore when you are without you can turn to the resources within to satisfy your needs. This is more than money and material resources, which only meets the physical needs - material resources cannot meet the emotional and spiritual needs.

Synchronise the inner and outer life

The difference between the inner and outer is what makes living a strain. The inner needs to be in synchrony with the outer. Without this synchronicity one will always feel false. So look to God to enable you to harmonise the internal and external. For a time the gap gives you a sense of falseness but this falseness is what will enable you to choose the real. Be vulnerable for in weakness will be your strength. So don't give in to the voice that condemns you. Rather listen to the voice of God who says I can do it - I can do all things through Christ who strengthens me. It's Christ's work to strengthen me and equip me. Yes, there are different facets of Christ's work. The variety is enormous. So don't be blinded by the emphasis on those who only highlight one area.

Balance in all areas

Life is a balance. Cults, occults, fanatics and extremists will always major in one doctrine at the expense of others. God is not like that. He is God of your body, mind and spirit. It is man who can't balance the whole and finds satisfaction in one area. It is very few who are able to balance their lives. The focus on one area gives a kind of energy that releases a stimulant or addictive substance - maybe endorphins that keep you focused. This is what stimulants do. Being stimulated from within enables one to be focused but also to be true to oneself. Focus is necessary at times to achieve a particular task. However, it is when this task takes over ones life that one loses balance. This kind of imbalance is seen in every aspect of life. This is why one needs to work as part of a team to bring balance. This is part of life. One is part of a whole. One cannot live on an island for oneself. Others maybe able accommodate for a time. God has called you to serve. It is this attitude of service that will enable you to see others as part of the whole. Just as the body has different parts so also in the family, group, and team - it is only as each one takes responsibility for the whole that harmony will take place. It is the family that comes first. So also in my relationship with God, it is only when I give all to Him and trust in Him that I become whole. Otherwise I will be satisfied in my narrow area of interest. The danger of having individual goals is that there is a price to pay unless the goal is serving the group or the larger goal. Goals give direction but they must be in the context with something else - family, work. If it is not in the context of the whole then the goal will not synchronise with the whole. Therefore when I submit all my plans to God - I enable Him to enable me to fit into His overall plan. In this context I am part of Gods overall plan. I accept that I am a part and God will enable me to fulfil that part. So whatever His calling, He will enable me to do as I keep my eyes on Him and do my part to be His representative in fulfilling His plan.

Worship

Worship in spirit and in truth. This is only possible in the Spirit. This is true worship. There are many levels of worship - that's why you see many levels of operations of the spirit. A spiritual man does not judge by the external. Judge by the spirit. Just as there are different degrees of development so also there are different degrees of worship. So one does not judge in terms of outward measures but by the inward state of the heart. The external is based on the senses. The internal - no one can see and only the spiritual man can judge the things of the spirit. So I need to seek the things of the spirit to appreciate others. It is so easy to judge in the flesh the things of the spirit. The positive attitude is that others are at different levels of growth and development so accept them for where they are and encourage them in their area of endeavour. The flesh envies others work because it is a threat. God has called each one to a place and each one has got their own troubles. Difference always leads to defensiveness. So let down your defences - they only serve as a barrier and keep you distanced from others. A man who is prepared to learn will grow and become connected with others.

Defensiveness cripples

Defence keeps you from others, safe in yourself but at a great cost to you because you have shut off from experiencing the joy of living. Increased defensiveness leads to a crippling of the inner child till one is just a thing in existence. This pursuit for material things makes one into a thing. Therefore change course. Do not be caught up in the same struggle - for money will suddenly disappear and what you have left is a shell. The deep things of life are not in what you see - they are in character. This character is what enables you to operate from within when you are without. The spiritual nature of people who live in poverty is because they have learnt to live from within. They enjoy the simple things of life. While in the world there is need for higher stimulation from external sources. No, God has not called you to this. God has called you to build His Kingdom from within. This is only possible through total surrender to Him in the spirit. Then in His fullness, experience the abundance there is in Him, and minister to the needs of others. Just listen to the Spirit as you listen to others. Clarity comes in and the word you speak forth suddenly enlightens the mind and heals the body and the soul. This is the work of the spirit. Not in the external but in the operations within. So do not be threatened by the external but be strong from within. God will show you each day what you have to do and will provide you with the wisdom you need to do it. So rejoice and be glad. You are special and called to a special purpose. Broken to be a vessel of power and glory to magnify His glorious and wonderful Name.

Heavenly manna

Manna from heaven. This is what I need daily to refresh my soul. Earthly manna only satisfies the flesh. It is the Holy Spirit that provides the heavenly manna. This manna is the Word of God. God speaks to your spirit through His Spirit. This is life to the spirit and health to the soul and the body. So seek this heavenly manna daily in your life. This manna sustains not only your life now but forever. The words of life are for now and forever. Knowledge that you gain through your senses is just for the now. So feed on the heavenly manna. Everything else pales into insignificance as you feast on the heavenly manna. Trust Him always for He is worthy of your love. He is the One who will count you as present. He is the bright and morning star. The God of all ages - the ever present One - mighty to save - mighty to redeem. Hallelujah, God is alive.

Trust is the now word to you. Trust God who has called you to a place of power and strength. Do not trust man who wavers like the wind. Only a person whose feet are on the Rock of Ages will be able to stand. No man is able to stand without the strength of God. All men are fallible. So put your trust in God. Exalt His Name. Jehovah God is your strength. Now go and magnify His Name.

Reach out for more

As the opening of the leaves reveals the flower - so as you walk out in faith God reveals the truth. So stretch out. Don't be limited by your success. It is as you reach out that more will be supplied to you. This is faith. Sitting down will not release His resources. It is in facing the mountain that results in victory. As you face the mountain the mountain becomes smaller. As you practice, as you learn and relearn. As you memorise, and recall - so you will gain ground. Trust in the Lord to bring to your remembrance what you need to know. Don't be taken up with performance anxiety. Believe that you know best what is required. Be prepared to be corrected and challenged. This way you learn from experience what is good. Having a long-term view enables you to see things in perspective. Don't waste your time on things that will not change. So decide on your priorities. Maximum leverage is possible in areas of minimum change. Where change is possible it is just a push that is required. Common sense therapy. Don't recourse to explorations and theorising when what is required is so simple and straightforward. Any situation is soluble - it is a matter of finding the right people who have the answers to the situation. God will guide you to the right people. Remember when you have entrusted control of your life to Him that He is in control to make things happen that will stand you up. No crisis is too big a crisis for Him. It is your response that makes a crisis a disaster or a place for change and creativity. Resist the move to allow bullies and manipulators to control your life. Don't give in to them. Rather stand your ground firmly. You are called to be light and salt. So stand and be the light. Do not be threatened by the forces that can threaten or control you. You belong to God. You are the head and not the tail. You are to lead by example. Open up your mouth and speak the liberating word. This word will enable you to release the captive, release yourself into abundance. Your body will respond to the now Word. So wait for His Word always. Any discomfort or angry response is a reaction of the flesh. Wait and see how you feel after the initial reaction as you commit all to Him. He will then open up the way for you. It is important that you do so. For it is only what is brought to the light can survive the darkness. What is in the dark is hidden. So speak and do not fear. For you have been called to be light. This is where your strength will be - in weakness. Do not be afraid to be a fool for Christ for it is the foolish thing that He will glorify.

Open to the Spirit

The Lord comes and anoints whomever He pleases. All you need to do is be open to the movement of His Spirit. Just like the man beside the pool waited - so wait expectantly. This expectancy fuels your faith, which then taps into Gods mighty resources in heaven. There is supply unlimited for all your needs and for the whole world. Just like you need to go to the fuel pump to fill your tank so also you need to connect with God to be filled. All the distractions in this world - like TV saps you of spiritual energy. They are ready-made pictures and don't take any active involvement from you and you are exposed to a source that is of man and not of God. So what you connect with will determine the outcome of your life. If you choose to connect with God then you connect with the external source of wisdom. It is from within that God communicates. You may hear a lot of good messages and see a lot of videos but it is what happens within you that determines the outcome of your life. What you associate with may rub off on you but may not last. It is what you feed from within that enables you to do. You can't survive from the resources from without if the machinery within is dead. Food is for the stomach to digest the essential ingredients for life to be sustained. Food as such cannot sustain life. So if the organ within is not in order then the body begins to dysfunction because of lack of essential nutrients. So also all that you see and hear without is just that. It is what is processed within that results in life and action. A bit of good advice is not good until it is received and acted upon. Knowledge applied is what leads to life.

So connect with God and see how the Spirit when He has control over you will release the wisdom and the knowledge so you know that this is truly a work of God. So be patient and calm - convinced of this one thing that the God who has called you to act is with you to perform His wondrous work. He is Jehovah God. All you need to do is to flow with His Spirit. You are just an instrument of His peace - flow in Him. Determine to be completely sold out to Him - to be possessed by Him. Enjoy all His benefits and rejoice in Him. God has given you all things to enjoy. Rejoice and be glad for Jehovah lives forever. Your whole being will vibrate with the spirit of God within you. Signs and wonders will be seen because of the Spirit's presence within you. As you walk by faith - you will find that manifestations will occur that will astound you.

Total abandonment to the Lord

Selling all for Jesus. When you sell all that you possess then you are free of all things and live by faith alone. These things you have are for the family - for them to enjoy. To live by faith alone is to live each day on the resources of heaven and to receive by faith all that you need. To come to this position of total abandonment to the Lord is a place of rest and peace. The world goes after the things of the world. This is right to do but you are not of this world. When you get involved or associated with the things of the world then you become like them. However, you are called to be separate from the world to influence it. You are part of this world but not of it. If heaven is in you then you become a holy influence on others. This is what it means to be salt. When you look back you know it is by faith that you received. So it will be as you look forward. Riches, wisdom, knowledge will be given to you as you look up and out to the One who will lead you. Today you can have all things you need. Today is a new day. So look to Him. Let all the negatives of the flesh fade away or fall away as you look to Him. Trust in Him alone. He is present to lift you up. Yes, as you give up all things He will come to bless you with His things to see you over from day to day. See how rested you feel. No pressures - just rest. Enjoy His rest. Why go after the things of this world. Enjoy the simple pleasures - do not try to imitate or copy what is seen by the world as good. Rather look to what you enjoy - the simple things. Trying to be like the world is to be unnatural. Be natural - as if living in the Kingdom of God. This is what you enjoy and this is what is natural to you. This is life to you. Yes you have to live in this world but the Kingdom of God is within you. So shed off the things of this world. Judgment and wisdom comes from above. There is no one who can satisfy like Him. You are in Him - so live naturally like Him. Why get embroiled in the issues of daily life when eternal life itself is your portion. Enjoy this life. Why seek for what is of this world when the pearl of great price lives in you. So just come empty and live this life of faith. The more negatives you experience the more you will experience His love. The positive will thrive in the negative. That is why you have been put here - like a sun to shine in the darkness. So shine. My burden is lifted - so no more look for the praises of man but for the glory of God. Lord, come and fill me with your light. I know in part. I choose to live a pure life that the glory of God maybe seen in me. I am just an instrument of His peace to water a thirsty land. I will give what I have that others may enjoy the freedom I enjoy.

Transparency

Commit all to Jesus. This is the way to purify things and let Him have control. It is when you take control that things go wrong. When you commit all to Him then you can be assured that you will not manipulate or try and do it your way. This is to let go and let God or in other words let others grow. This is true love. All other kinds of love are manipulative or tend to serve ones own needs. These are done in indirect ways. Your talk and walk are subtlely deceptive - always having your own agenda and not what is best for the others. People therefore become guarded knowing not what to expect. When you commit all to Him - you become transparent. Others may not be like that. In the world, people put on masks as a defence. But a truly mature man is not fooled by their masks. He sees them as defences to keep others away or deceived. All are vulnerable so need to hide behind status, position, cars, homes etc. However these are all cover ups for the real thing. People are longing for deliverance from these outward faces. The psychotic escapes from the pressures and stresses of the world by listening to the imaginations of his own mind, which oppress him or deceive him. The neurotic on the other hand deceives himself and does not know his real self anymore, which has been buried under layers of defences. The pain and the suffering are endless. Yet, by committing all to Jesus there is deliverance - deliverance from a self made prison to wonderful liberty - full of joy, love, faith, zeal and power. What an exchange. Yet the only way is through absolute surrender - death through offering my life up as a living sacrifice to Him. He then works it out in me. It is not through my works. I just need to walk by faith - committing all to Him and He then works it out in me. In all areas big and small - His Spirit cleanses and empowers as I commit all to Him. It is only in the areas where I choose to hold on that I will feel fear, guilt and pain. I own or possess nothing. All God has given me is for me to enjoy. I am nothing - He is everything. Because He is everything, I can now sit back and enjoy all things. No pressure is too much for me. Tomorrow I may die - so I will enjoy today - the pain and the joys. I live that others may enjoy the love and peace of God as they eat of the fruits of my life.

Surrender to Jesus - key to exorcise demon of control

Christ has apprehended me. He has purchased me with His own blood. He has redeemed me and saves me. Now I commit all to Him. He fills me up and He protects me. I just surrender to Him. Surrender leads to change. Control leads to conflict. So each time you see yourself in conflict - surrender the situation to Jesus. Let Him have control. In this way He will take control. The devil will have no say or control. The devil will flee as you resist by giving control to Jesus. Every time the flesh rises against the spirit - surrender to the spirit. Use your will. Commit your will to Christ. He is the Alpha and Omega. He is the risen one - the Almighty resurrected Christ. So open up - see how He will lead you by His Spirit. As you let go it is as if there is nothing to resist and the rest follows. This is the way forward. There is an eternal struggle going on in the world. It is a spirit of rebellion. This rebellious spirit can only fight against rebellion. This spirit will be defeated through love. There is no other way. Christ did not win the war against Satan by fighting Him but by submitting to the Father. This is the only way to overcome. Set others free by allowing them to be themselves. This is your task or role - to enable others to express themselves and not to judge. In this way you free yourself to be yourself. You have chosen to follow Christ. If you want others to accept you then you have to accept others and their ways. This is the only way of love - acceptance. People are people. They will resist any kind of control. Children to adults. The way forward is to ignore the trivial and pay attention to the important.

God chose to love the sinner. Love goes to the ultimate and love never resists except evil but even here love overcomes evil with good. This is the paradox. The greatest form of love is to lay oneself down. Evil cannot stand the force of light so resist or overcome evil with good. A negative situation is an opportunity to sow love. Love is the answer - positive, possibility thinking and action lead to solutions. So the mountains of negativity are razed to the ground as the positive power of God fills you. You can have all of God only when you give all to God and empty yourself daily of all of self.

Purity

Living a life of sinless purity. This is only possible in the fullness of the Holy Spirit. God fills me so that I can live this life of purity from within. It is purity within that leads to pure action. When my eye is pure - I see all things as pure. It is my own greed, jealousy and envy that lead me to see things as impure. I am me - born in sin - yet I have been delivered from sin through the sacrificial death of Jesus. Jesus died that I maybe free. I am free to be. It is Gods power in me that leads to redemption. Redemption is the saving of a soul from sins control. God is calling me to live life that is in accordance or harmony with my eternal redemption. I am destined for heaven. That is where I am headed for. Now my life on earth must lead me to forsake all things that will keep me to be true to the end of my life. I will synchronise my activities, hope, dreams, desires, and actions to this one goal. All the superficial things that I see and have are nothing to that which is internal and eternal. I come present to Jesus in me that I may receive the good things of the Spirit. The good things of the spirit keep me, preserves me from the longings of the flesh. I am so I can. I am a man of God. God indwells me. I speak to Him. I reject all thoughts and feelings that are contrary to His will. I see them as attacks from the flesh or the devil. I go in and dwell in the bosom of Jesus and receive comfort and peace. These attacks are there to make me stronger and I rejoice not only in the abundant life I experience now in Him but also in the fellowship of His suffering. The two go hand in hand. Because I am in Him I see the sufferings as His opportunities. If Jesus forsook the way of the Cross then he would have had to compromise with the devil. Rather He stood against evil and therefore He suffered. True change comes as I commit all to Jesus. I will be challenged. Only someone who has something to stand for will be challenged. So do not be surprised if you are challenged. In that time I shall give you the words and feelings, power and strength that comes from the Spirit. The Spirit in you is the one who will enable you to do. This is the new word to you. Wait and see how the Lord will move to strengthen and liberate you. He is interested in you. Don't be pushed to do things that are not of Him. So wait. Be content in where you are at present. Life is a journey. So enjoy all you have now. Work on clarifying your feelings. Yes, wild horses will come but see this as an opportunity to direct your energies into that, which is good. Resist the temptation to give in to temporary pleasures. Build on the lasting works of unity, harmony, love, joy and peace. Money cannot buy these things. Be strong and very courageous. God is with you and in you. This is the assurance you have. So rejoice today in Him and be glad.

CONVERTING YOUR NEGATIVES INTO POSITIVES THROUGH LOVE AND FORGIVENESS

Good can come out of negativity. Negativity is just one side of the coin. Love and hate are opposite sides of the same coin. Where there is hate remember there is love as well. The capacity to love is balanced by the capacity to hate. This is why conflict in relationships enables a person to forgive and love again. Where there is no forgiveness then hate takes control and love is repressed. Love is released as one learns to forgive. Where there is no conflict then hate is being repressed. Hate then converts into physical symptoms. So do not be afraid of negativity. Underneath is the potential for positive feelings. A person who is resistive to negative feelings will not be able to sustain long term relationships. The capacity to love is directly related to the capacity to forgive. The two must go together. Throughout history this has been the case. God saw the sin and negativity in the world. Forgiveness came through the Cross and love and power was released through it. So also relationships are sealed as negativity is converted to love through forgiveness.

There is fear in negativity. The fear is not based in love. Where love is the platform then all negativity will not be allowed to take root. So walk in forgiveness at all times. Negative emotions and images and thoughts will be aroused but walking in forgiveness will enable love to heal the wounds. A person who continuously breeds and harbours negativity will be bound by it. Praying in tongues enables you to overcome by allowing Gods thoughts, images and feelings to come in and heal. Therefore understanding this is part of the solution but walking in it is the solution.

Breaking patterns of the past is to walk in forgiveness to day. Ask the Holy Spirit to anoint you with love and forgiveness. A person who is filled with love cannot but forgive. God says you are filled. Now you can love and forgive. In this way you set yourself free and others too who you are related to. Do not walk in the counsel of men but of God as you are a free agent of God. You are not bound by the laws of man because you walk in the counsel of God. His counsel liberates you from the impositions of the law. For there is no law above the law of love. So when you walk in love and forgiveness then you walk in the light. Each and every conflict is an opportunity to love and forgive. Where there is no love and forgiveness then conflict and negativity will paralyse you and keep you bound.

So rejoice in the conflict - for underneath is the opportunity to greater release and freedom. It's like a boulder that needs to be moved out of the way so that the light can come in. Each step in the journey of life is a hurdle. Each step is a challenge to rise up to higher realms. This means conflict. Progress involves change, conflict and growth. Where there is no growth, there is no challenge, no conflict. Conflict is a positive arena for change and growth to occur. It brings out the best and worst in people. Surviving conflict is to cement a relationship. When people walk away from conflictual situations then people lose out and do not learn from it. So look at conflicts as opportunities to learn, grow and be strong. It arouses the most basic emotions in you but these need to be controlled by the higher emotions of love, self-control and forgiveness. Praying in the spirit will enable you to deal with these negative emotions and subdue them and live in the positive resurrection power of God. It's this that enables you to change the negative to the positive. No one learns through positive experiences alone. One learns more through the negative experiences of life - for it is the negative that brings out the positive - just like the oyster is irritated to produce the pearl.

INDEX

- Abundant living — 201
- Acceptance of self and others — 85
- Acceptance — 85
- Adam's sin - Jesus death — 177
- Addictions — 90
- Adolescence — 33
- Adolescent rebellion — 34
- Affirmation — 158
- Anger and anxiety/depression — 43
- Anger — 27
- Anxiety - Man's Worst Enemy — 28
- Asking questions — 41
- Attachment to God — 183
- Attitudes — 91
- Balance in all areas — 215
- Battles — 184
- Becoming what you imagine — 59
- Being one — 60
- Belief systems — 56
- Believe in yourself — 99
- Bondage — 196
- Breaking through — 207
- Celebrate difference — 40
- Change of attitude — 93
- Change — 36
- Change — 44
- Change — 122
- Changed into His image — 214
- Changing old patterns — 50
- Character building — 83
- Childhood experiences — 130

- Children and defences — 65
- Children and parents — 20
- Choices — 212
- Christ in me — 212
- Christ our reference point — 152
- Coming in touch with ones feelings — 54
- Communication — 16
- Confidence in self — 98
- Conflict — 100
- Conformity — 104
- Connecting behaviours and emotions — 139
- Contentment — 165
- Converting your negatives into positives — 226
- Coping — 71
- Creating difference — 39
- Creator God — 197
- Cross and salvation — 173
- Crucify the flesh — 162
- Dealing with negative thoughts — 63
- Death brings life into focus — 215
- Defence mechanisms — 15
- Defences — 65
- Defensiveness cripples — 217
- Defensiveness — 65
- Depending on God for all things — 136
- Deprive old patterns of attention — 49
- Deprived children — 22
- Destiny — 184
- Difference and beauty — 131
- Discerning the spirit — 211
- Don't despair — 114
- Emotional independence — 139
- Emotional pain — 22
- Emotional Problems — 113
- Emotionally free — 78
- Empowered from within — 135
- Emptiness — 60

- ♦ Expectations 81
- ♦ Experience 73
- ♦ Facing your fears 75
- ♦ Faith imagination 193
- ♦ Faith in action 136
- ♦ Faith in God 182
- ♦ Faith in Jesus Christ 64
- ♦ Faith in self in God 208
- ♦ Faith in the glorified life of Christ 180
- ♦ Faith overcomes fear 103
- ♦ Faith walk 205
- ♦ Faith 191
- ♦ False guilt 74
- ♦ False self and feelings 158
- ♦ Family first 123
- ♦ Family therapy 38
- ♦ Fantasy and idealised relationships 82
- ♦ Feelings and communication 18
- ♦ Feelings 54
- ♦ Fixed in purpose 107
- ♦ Focusing on solutions 123
- ♦ Forces of good and evil 168
- ♦ Frames of reference 102
- ♦ Freedom in Christ 66
- ♦ Friendship 116
- ♦ Friendship 90
- ♦ Giving as sowing 129
- ♦ Giving till it hurts 207
- ♦ Goal setting 121
- ♦ God is in control 196
- ♦ God is in control 111
- ♦ Gods love 141
- ♦ Gods salvation 157
- ♦ Going beyond the problems 125
- ♦ Gratefulness 198
- ♦ Groups 25
- ♦ Habits 124

- Head and heart unity 80
- Hearing Gods now voice 183
- Heavenly manna 218
- Heavenly wisdom 183
- Helping others to help themselves 119
- His life -not beliefs 173
- Hitting rock bottom 136
- Holy Spirit the conductor 191
- Holy Spirit 187
- Humility 186
- Identifications 155
- Imagination 192
- Imprisoned by our past 49
- In Christ 147
- Independence and serving one another 53
- Influences 91
- Integrate your values with your goals 109
- Integrity 113
- Interdependency 71
- Introspection 61
- Investing in others 195
- Investing in others 122
- Issues and feelings 23
- Issues 51
- Jesus - our standard 154
- Jesus Christ and Him crucified 185
- Jesus is Lord 167
- Keep to the right 163
- Knowledge and change 37
- Knowledge of man is limited 56
- Labelling 86
- Laughter 119
- Leaders 99
- Liberty in Jesus 164
- Live in the now 147
- Love and humility 187
- Love gives and gives 128

- Love is above difference — 194
- Love key to release — 105
- Love — 193
- Love, faith and sex — 126
- Loving others-judging their thoughts — 125
- Loving self, loving others — 115
- Man is a spirit being — 177
- Masks — 30
- Maturity — 138
- Mental phenomena — 14
- Mind sets — 93
- Motivation — 84
- Moving in faith — 203
- New life in Jesus — 156
- Nuggets of Truth — 150
- Old self and self — 70
- On being — 154
- Open to the Spirit — 220
- Opening up to Gods resources — 87
- Operating in faith — 123
- Opinions — 107
- Organisations and change — 37
- Overcoming faith — 210
- Paradigms shifts — 97
- Perceptions — 32
- Perceptions — 96
- Persistence — 117
- Personal relationship with God — 172
- Positive attitude — 92
- Positive thinking — 95
- Power of the tongue — 179
- Powerful change induction — 127
- Prayer and imagination — 132
- Prayer of renunciation — 198
- Prayer power — 189
- Prayer — 189
- Praying in tongues — 134

- Preparing for success — 112
- Pressing on — 108
- Principles of the Kingdom — 174
- Problem solving — 41
- Problem solving — 103
- Problems as opportunities — 118
- Programming for success — 106
- Projections — 26
- Projective identification — 27
- Prophetic word — 214
- Prosperity — 105
- Punitive superego — 24
- Purity — 224
- Reach out for more — 219
- Reactions — 30
- Reactions — 120
- Regression and feelings — 19
- Relationships — 31
- Relationships — 67
- Religions of the world — 68
- Remedy — 181
- Repentance key to forgiveness — 156
- Resistance to change — 100
- Rest in Christ — 149
- Roles — 25
- Roles — 62
- Saintliness and sinfulness — 160
- Sanctification — 69
- Sanctifying our bodies daily for the Holy Spirit — 210
- Satanic arrows — 185
- Secrets — 52
- Security — 91
- Seeing with the eyes of Jesus — 155
- Seeking Gods way — 158
- Self centred to other centred — 133
- Self centred life style — 67
- Self esteem — 88

- Self sacrifice — 199
- Selfishness — 170
- Significance and love — 130
- Sin and repentance — 159
- Sin and salvation — 160
- Sin controls you — 161
- Sin of introspection — 159
- Sin — 87
- Sinful flesh — 161
- Solutions — 39
- Speaking Gods truth in love — 208
- Splits and togetherness — 25
- Stop judging others — 107
- Strategy — 101
- Success in God — 111
- Suffering — 164
- Superficial needs vas. deeper needs — 76
- Surrender to Jesus-key to exorcise demon of control — 223
- Synchronise the inner and outer life — 215
- Systems change — 37
- Systems theory — 38
- Taking up ones cross — 178
- The Anorexic Stance — 34
- The Child and Family — 21
- The larger picture — 38
- The Lord is in control — 46
- The Lord is my Shepherd — 134
- The neurotics prison — 89
- The power of the Cross — 179
- The system binds — 120
- Theories and theories — 63
- Think — 95
- Thoughts — 63
- Total abandonment to the Lord — 221
- Total dependence on God — 137
- Transparency — 222
- Trinity working together — 180

- True integration — 81
- Trust in God — 202
- Truth is in a person — 167
- Two competing forces — 137
- Unblocking the flow — 110
- Unity in ones belief system — 59
- Values — 212
- Victims — 32
- Victorious living — 195
- Vision — 209
- Visualisation — 190
- Voices of the past — 163
- Voices of the past — 48
- Walking in the spirit — 205
- Walking with Jesus — 206
- Whole body filling — 52
- Wisdom — 45
- Word of God — 176
- Worship — 217
- Yoked to Christ — 200

Printed in Great Britain
by Amazon.co.uk, Ltd.,
Marston Gate.